DAILY TELEGRAPH
GUIDE TO INCOME TAX

The Daily Telegraph
Guide to
Income Tax

new revised edition

prepared by a
Daily Telegraph
Tax Correspondent

COLLINS·LONDON AND GLASGOW

William Collins Sons & Co. Ltd.
London & Glasgow

First published 1974
Completely revised and reset edition 1977
Completely revised and reset edition 1978
Fully updated edition 1979

© *Daily Telegraph* 1974, 1978
ISBN 0 00 434169 4
Printed in Great Britain

CONTENTS

INTRODUCTORY NOTE

Between the publication of the *Daily Telegraph Guide to Income Tax* in 1974 and the 1977 edition a great deal of new tax legislation was passed. So much so that the ordinary taxpayer who could not afford professional assistance was confronted by ever-increasing problems.

In these circumstances the author and the publishers decided that the 1977 edition should not merely be revised and updated but should be completely redesigned and rewritten. The success of this new version amply vindicated the decision to offer a redesigned book, and also encouraged us to present the book in the same format for the 1978 and 1979 edition, basing the approach on the actual forms the taxpayer has to cope with. The present edition has been revised and updated by one of the *Daily Telegraph*'s professional Tax Correspondents.

1

COMPLETING AN INCOME TAX RETURN

There is a variety of income tax return forms. Some ask for more information than others. It depends upon the number of sources of income and the degree of complexity surrounding one's general tax situation.

When discussing the completion of an income tax return, I think one should have in mind the needs of the ordinary taxpayer. The company chairman, the man in big business, the so-called tycoon—however one describes him—will usually be opting out of the tax scene in favour of the professional tax adviser.

I have thus selected form 11 for analysis, because this series was designed some years ago in an endeavour to produce something basically as simple as our complicated tax law will allow. It asks for income from every source, plus allowances claimed, in as concise a manner as may be found. I am referring to form 11 (1979) which is headed 'Income tax year 1979/80' and calls for income arising in the year ended 5th April 1978.

The Allowances section
On the reasonable assumption that it is the fervent wish of every taxpayer that he or she be required to pay the minimum annual amount of tax which the law demands, it is of the utmost importance that every allowance which is considered to be due should be claimed.

When completing this section, it should be borne in mind that you are claiming allowances for the year following that for which the income in the return is required. On receipt of the return, the tax office is thus given the opportunity of adjusting the coding already issued, or of issuing a correct coding in the first place where they had been late off the mark.

For the record—as if you didn't know—an allowance is a deduction from total income, which makes the taxable income that much lower. In short, the greater the total of allowances claimed, the less tax there will be to pay. Conversely, the tax *saving* by reference to allowances claimed can be calculated. Those who pay tax for 1978/79 at the basic rate of 33% on at least the amount of the married man's personal allowance, £1535, save £506·55 as a result of claiming it. A tycoon whose highest rate of tax is, say, 70% would be saving as much as £1074·50.

I have set out, under the chapter *Checking a notice of coding*, the various allowances which may be claimed for 1978/79. In return form 11, the spaces for three of the various allowances are set out on page 1 and for the rest of them on page 4. Let it be said, at this stage, that if you make no claim at all for any of the possible allowances, you will nonetheless be given the allowance of a single person—£985 for 1978/79.

There is one allowance, and one only, which the taxpayer is not required to claim. This is the single personal allowance. This minimum entitlement given in a notice of coding has caused many a taxpayer to wake up to the fact that not only has he a wife and four children but that for the last three years at least he has, in spite of reminders, omitted to lodge his annual returns.

One assumes that the married man has become accustomed to inserting his wife's Christian names in the first of the allowance sections on page 1. This ensures his £1535 personal allowance for 1978/79, but, if he, or his wife, is, or will be, 65 during 1978/79, he must put a cross in the box in the second section to indicate to the tax office that he was born before 6th April 1914. This puts him in a better tax position than the younger man because his personal allowance becomes an age allowance of £1300 if single, or £2075 if married.

The section relating to child allowance is simple enough, and I have given you on page 65 a formula if you want to calculate how much your children are saving you in tax. The thing to remember about this section, however, is the necessity to keep the tax office in the picture with regard to children of 16 or over. Are they going on to technical college or university? If so, for how long? How much is it estimated that they will be earning during holidays?

The important thing is to anticipate, as far as possible, any enquiries from the tax office. If you can keep them up-to-date concerning your older children's circumstances, the tax authorities, in turn, will keep your code number up-to-date, so that there is no large underpayment or overpayment of tax at the end of the year.

The column headed 'Child's earnings and other income' is an important one. Your child or children may, for example, be entitled to income from a settlement, and the *gross* income is the figure required. This may vary from year to year, and the trustees of the settlement should be asked for the figures. If they cannot be obtained in time for the completion of the return, don't hold it up, but advise your tax office of the figures as soon as possible afterwards. You will notice that an estimate for the year ahead is necessary, and it should be possible to give a reasonably accurate figure.

Turning over to page 4, we find the spaces for claiming the rest of the allowances. My advice here is that it is worth spending a little time reading through the wording within all these sections very carefully. Those who are getting on in years may have become used to drawing a long diagonal line right across page 4. It may be, however, that a claim for one or more of these allowances has suddenly become possible. If you realize that it has, read carefully the note applicable to it by reference to the first column on page 4 in the Tax Return Guide 1978/79 pages 7 and 8.

If it should happen that you find that you have been missing out on an allowance for a year or two, don't worry. Complete the appropriate section under Allowances and write a note to the Inspector of Taxes with the return to the effect that you should have been claiming for, say, a dependent relative since 1974/75. He will probably send you, in due course, a separate claim form for the particular allowance, and this has merely to be completed, signed, and returned. A refund of tax may then be expected.

As long as the Inspector is satisfied that the appropriate conditions have been fulfilled, he will admit and accept a claim for six years back. For example, a claim for the year 1973/74, and perhaps for some or all of the subsequent years, must be in the hands of the tax office by the 5th April 1980. From this example, you can work out the deadline for any back year which you may have missed.

Before we leave the Allowances section of the annual return, it is relevant to mention that a refund of tax may, in some cases, be obtainable on the strength of the lodgment of the annual return—

or even before it is lodged. This is discussed under 'Completing an income tax claim'.

INCOME

Generally

At the time of going to press it is not possible for me to discuss a return form of later vintage than the form 11 (1978). This calls for income from all sources which arose in the year ended 5th April 1978 although, as I have indicated, the allowances claimed relate to 1978/79.

Before we get on to the actual completion of the various sections on pages 2 and 3, I would say how important it is to keep a copy of the annual income tax return. Personally, I always write out my return on a plain sheet of paper, and only when I am completely satisfied with it do I fill in the form itself. I find that this avoids any alterations in the finished article, and I have automatically provided myself with a copy to enable me to deal with any questions which the Inspector of Taxes may see fit to put to me.

There is another general point worth mentioning. Inland Revenue forms are not exactly noted for the amount of space which they provide for the verbal details relating to income, outgoings, and capital gains or losses. This drawback can be overcome in many instances by detailed statements lodged with the return. Thus the words 'see separate statement', and the amount, in many of the sections will suffice. If these statements can be typed, so much the better. This ensures clarity for the tax office and copies for you.

Trade, profession or vocation

The first section on page 2 calls for the net income of those who, broadly speaking, work for themselves. Those within this category are distinctly in the minority, but the income which they show in the annual return is not only of their own making in the obvious sense, it is produced, as it were, for the purposes of the return, and the approval of the Inspector of Taxes, by a statement of account.

Although I have dealt with the preparation and layout of various accounts and statements in a separate chapter, I will mention here that the tax office expects an account which accurately reflects the net profit shown in the return. They may even ask for a certificate at the foot of it that it represents a true and accurate statement of receipts and outgoings for the year concerned. Furthermore, balancing charges and any deduction for capital allowances are also discussed within the same chapter.

Employments or offices

This is one of the simpler sections of the annual return. Those in employment will receive from their employers each year after the 5th April a statement on form P60 showing the total earnings of the year and the tax deducted under PAYE. The total will include all earnings whether or not you have changed your employment during the course of the tax year. If you have, you should show each employer's name and address in the particulars column, but one total taken from the P60 will be sufficient for the purpose of the return.

I should perhaps mention here that where a taxpayer's only income is from employment, an annual return is not necessarily issued every year. The tax office knows that the situation is fairly static, but if further allowances become due during a tax year, the tax office should be advised immediately, so that the code number may be appropriately adjusted.

The rest of the section is reasonably straightforward by reference to the subheadings and the relevant notes in the tax return guide. Benefits such as a car, the running expenses, the value of accommodation, and so on may have subsequently to be justified. On the other hand, the Inspector may not assess them as earnings where he has information from the employer which indicates their admissibility.

Social Security pensions and benefits

I have given you most of the information which you require to complete this section in the chapter on the notice of coding. Don't forget to put an 'X' in the box if you have a wife who contributed towards a pension in her own right. If she did so, your total Social Security pensions will be more than would have been the case had she not contributed.

The subsection calling for widow's and other benefits embraces quite a number of different kinds of Social Security payments. More of these are exempt from tax (and should thus be excluded from the return) than are taxable. If, therefore, you are in doubt, and want to save your own time and that of others, please refer to Note 17 in the tax return guide, because it reveals all.

Many taxpayers become entitled to the state pension at some point within the tax year. I always recommend here that one keeps a careful note of each weekly amount drawn. Add these receipts up at the following 5th April, and you have the figure for inclusion in your next tax return. This is of particular interest to widows, who receive a larger-than-normal weekly sum for the first 26 weeks. These larger weekly amounts may spill over into part of the next tax year, and a careful record of the weekly receipts in these cases in the tax year following widowhood is also important.

Other pensions

Those who receive a pension from a former employer are in a similar position from the point of view of the completion of the annual income tax return as the person who has not reached pensionable age, and is in employment. The ex-employers will issue a form P60 at the close of each tax year, and the gross pension for inclusion in the return will be shown thereon.

You will notice that 'other pensions' includes a war widow's pension. From 1976/77 onwards, the long-overdue good news is that one half only of a war widow's own pension is exempt in calculating her taxable income. It should be noted, however, that the total pension should be inserted in the return. The tax office will—or should—omit half of it in their calculation of the taxable income, and, in due course, the widow should check that they have done so.

There are cases where war widows receive an allowance in respect of a child or children. If this allowance has been granted by the Secretary of State for Social Services it is also exempt. Where, however, the allowance is paid under the National Insurance scheme, it is taxable, and must be included in the return. Those in doubt about the source should check with the authority from whom the pension is received.

This section calls for pensions from abroad and they should *not* be included in the section lower down on page 2 which requires untaxed *income* from abroad. You should enter the whole of the foreign pension, although, as I have indicated in another chapter, only 90% (or, in some cases, only 50%) will be taxable. You may, however, be entitled to credit for any foreign tax suffered on it, and full particulars to your tax office, on a separate sheet of paper if necessary, will ensure that you obtain your legal entitlement.

Property

Generally

In a way, this section is different from all the others to be found in the income side of the annual return. Its three columns call for gross income, expenses, and net income. The quirk here is that the net income in the third column is really the gross income for tax purposes because it is the figure in the third column which, in due course, attracts any tax liability. It is thus part of the tax-payer's gross income which forms part of the total income.

I think it may therefore be said that there will normally be a statement of account in support of income returned under the heading of Property. This applies particularly to lettings, and I have referred to this matter, where necessary, under the various subsections. This means that where there is an accompanying statement which throws out a figure of net income from property, this figure may be inserted in the last column (under 'self' or 'wife' as appropriate), and in the particulars column will appear 'see attached statement'.

Lettings

Normally, it is no longer necessary to put any figure in this section concerning a property which you own and occupy. Gone are the bad old days when one was assessed under Schedule A on a notional annual value representing the rent which could be expected from your property were it to be let in the open market. In the majority of cases, therefore, the answer to this section is NONE.

I say normally because, exceptionally, you may be letting— either furnished or unfurnished—a room or rooms in the property which you own and which you mostly occupy. This produces income—unless, of course, you are of a kindly nature which allows your mother-in-law or whoever to make a bedsitter of one of your rooms without payment.

Payment for the occupation of a room or rooms in your house is income for tax purposes. Not earned income, but taxable income nonetheless. Those who do let a room or rooms in their houses, or own another house which is let, will find detailed instructions under 'Lettings' within the chapter on the preparation of various statements. If you study these instructions I am hopeful that you will then know the amount which should be inserted against 'Lettings'—whether unfurnished or furnished.

Having said this, I am not unmindful of the situation where a taxpayer may be letting properties in a big way. Even so, it is very rare indeed for an Inspector of Taxes to admit that a business is being conducted whereby the net profit is earned income, and thus occupying the first section on page 2 of the return.

Ground rents

This is, of course, a subheading relating to leasehold property. The ground landlord of such a property is normally in receipt of a ground rent. He may be ground landlord of a large number of properties which comprise an estate.

The annual ground rent received from one property, or the total of those from many, must be recorded under this subsection. I have not yet referred to the column headed 'Expenses' which serves the whole of the section on Property. The fact that the heading of the column includes '(enclose statement)' indicates, of course, that the tax office expects to have to examine quite a few items of expenditure from property generally—particularly that from lettings.

This is true, and that is why I referred to the preparation of statements of account for lettings. This will lead merely to an amount in figures for income and expenses in the return itself. I would suggest that one ground rent or so could not really be expected to cost anything to collect. On the other hand, a substantial income could quite easily attract admissible expenses. This could mean that an agent would be employed, and a copy of his periodical statements of account should be accepted by the Inspector of Taxes, with only the net assessable income in the return.

Land

This is another example where the income may be very small—derived, perhaps, from one field let out for grazing. There may be no expenses to set against a nominal rent. On the other hand, a substantial acreage (to be known, perhaps, as hectarage) may be let out for a substantial annual sum. The net receipts, as shown by a copy of an agent's account, should be acceptable to the Inspector of Taxes.

Interest not taxed before receipt

National and Trustee Savings Bank

I imagine that most of you know that, currently, the first £70 of both a husband's and wife's interest on *ordinary* accounts is exempt from tax. This does not apply to *investment* accounts, the interest from which is all taxable. The total interest from either ordinary or investment account must, however, be put into the return, but the Inspector will not tax any exempt part of it.

The interest from the above accounts is obtainable from the bank book, and you will find that National Savings Bank interest is credited annually at the 31st December, TSB interest is credited at 20th November. It is therefore a good plan to send the book up in January each year so that you have a note of the interest for inclusion in the next income tax return. The year's interest to the previous 31st December is acceptable to the Inland Revenue.

Other banks

This subsection calls for interest on a bank deposit account. The interest is normally credited twice a year on 30th June and 31st December. The total of these two credits is the amount to be included in the depositor's return of income for the year ended on the following 5th April. In my experience, if there happens to be a source of income which has been inadvertently overlooked, it is usually bank deposit interest. This may occur where a deposit account was opened during the tax year in question, and there was nothing from this source in the copy of the previous year's return to act as a reminder.

Banks have a duty to report any year's interest which is £25 or more, and where the taxpayer has omitted such interest he can expect a letter from the tax office asking him to consider whether income from all sources has, in fact, been disclosed. Nobody likes a sinister letter such as this, and I would suggest that bank deposit interest be the subject of a forward note in the file of every taxpayer who opens a deposit account at the bank.

Other sources

The interest on certain government loans and bonds is paid gross, and examples of these are set out in the particulars column. Those who have such investments should keep the advice counterfoils which come with the payments so that they are available for the completion of this subsection. I have also known County Councils to pay interest gross, and the occasional gross interest paid by stockbrokers on money held for future investment should also be reported here.

Untaxed income from abroad

This section is reserved solely for *unearned* income arising abroad. It is therefore confusing to the tax office to use this for foreign earnings, pension or income from an overseas trade. Any earned income from abroad goes into one or other of the first two sections on page 2.

You may ask what sort of foreign income is to be found in this section of the return. The answer is that the ordinary taxpayer would very seldom use it. You may suggest that dividends from overseas companies would be found here. Strictly speaking, this is correct, but overseas dividends are almost always collected in the first place by a paying agent—normally a bank.

Now the paying agent in these cases is authorized to deduct UK tax—and, in fact, does so. This means, in effect, that such dividends become *taxed income* from abroad, and there is no reason why they should not be included in a taxpayer's statement of dividends taxed at source. It would perhaps be more correct to call it interest taxed at source because dividends come with tax credits and the two categories should be the subject of separate statements to conform with the first two sections on page 3.

I think this is a situation where one should go by what is acceptable to the Inland Revenue. I have completed hundreds of returns and have always found that the totals from a separate statement of overseas dividends which have been taxed by a paying agent are acceptable under 'Other dividends' on page 3. Where, exceptionally, a dividend is received directly from an overseas company, it should, of course, be included as untaxed income from abroad—even though a measure of credit may have been given by the company for any overseas tax suffered.

The only other unearned untaxed income from abroad which comes to mind is rent collected by an agent from an overseas property or properties. A villa in Spain, for example, which, sensibly, is let whilst you are unable to enjoy it. The agent's account should embrace admissible outgoings and provide a figure for inclusion in the annual return. If any overseas tax is one of the outgoings in the account, obtain a receipt for it if possible, so that you may claim the appropriate credit against the UK tax otherwise found to be due. It may, however, be sufficient evidence if you forward a photostat copy of the agent's account with the return.

Interest from UK Building Societies

One of the simplest sections of the annual return. No problem at all—as long as you keep your half-yearly advices of interest in a place where you can find them when completing your return. One amount for the year per Society is enough, and there is normally room in this section without having to make a separate statement.

Dividends from UK companies and tax credits

In order to keep return form 11 down to a reasonable and manageable size this section has certainly taken a knock as far as availability of space is concerned. At an outside estimate, there is no room for more than two or three dividends each for husband and wife. It must therefore have been assumed—rightly, I suggest—that almost every taxpayer with investments would prepare a statement of them—if only as a record for himself. You will find instructions on this in the separate chapter devoted to the preparation of a variety of statements.

Other dividends, etc. already taxed

There is really no more room in this section than in the previous one. It has merely a different layout as regards husband and wife. Here again, I have discussed an appropriate form of statement in the relevant chapter. The only other point arising here is why there should be separate sections for two sources of income, both of which, in effect, have already suffered tax. The answer is that the designer of the return form has ensured, as far as possible, that the tax office will know, almost at a glance, the total gross amount of the investment income which has effectively suffered basic rate tax. The basic principle whereby the Inland Revenue has seen fit to separate the taxed investment income is this. Where dividends are received with tax credits, the gross income for all tax purposes is the total of the dividends plus the credits. On the other hand, where interest, etc., is taxed at source—in the way we used to know it with all dividends, interest, etc.—the gross amount is there for all to see, on the voucher, in fact, which accompanied the payment. It is not difficult to appreciate that a statement consisting of a hotchpotch of dividends, tax credits, gross income and tax deducted could take quite a time to unravel.

Any other profits or income

This is, of course, the 'sweeping-up' section. Its function is to cater for any source of income, however casual, for which no specific section has been provided elsewhere in the return. It is quite surprising how many odd items of taxable income there are. There is a sample of nearly twenty on page 4 of the Tax Return Guide, and I would not imagine that this embraces absolutely everything. My only advice, therefore, if you are in doubt over any casual receipt, is to consult this list. If the source is not there, you should have a word with your tax office.

OUTGOINGS

Expenses in employment

To be admissible as a deduction from earnings from employment, an expense must have been wholly, exclusively and necessarily incurred in the performance of the duties of such employment. This, of course, rather narrows down the field, but there are naturally a few items of expenditure which the taxpayer really believes should be allowed, but which the Inspector of Taxes would refuse. The Inspector's ruling is usually based on Case Law—of which there is a profusion on such a variety of expenditure as has emerged.

Fortunately, perhaps, the handful of expenses which are admissible against earnings are those which a taxpayer who is entitled to a deduction does not normally overlook. These include travelling expenses in the course of the duties, and subscriptions to professional bodies. I should perhaps mention here that superannuation contributions are an admissible deduction, but there is no longer any necessity to claim them under the above heading. Where applicable, they have already been deducted in arriving at a net earnings figure on the P60 issued by the employer.

Entertaining merits special mention because, in recent years, it has attracted very stringent rules regarding its admissibility. Expenditure on the *reasonable* entertainment of an *overseas* customer who is trading with your company is allowed. Otherwise, an allowance for entertainment is dependent upon the following two conditions being satisfied:

1. The expense for entertaining must have been disallowed for tax purposes against the tax liability of the employer.
2. The expenditure has to be justified by the taxpayer as having been necessarily incurred in the course of the duties of the employment—by such details to the Inspector as he requires.

Most of you, when completing the annual return, will be aware of expenses which you have been allowed against earnings over the past few years. If you find, however, that you have been missing out for a time on an item with which you now find the Inspector agrees, you should make a retrospective claim for a refund under the Error or Mistake provisions.

On the other hand, I hope I have given sufficient information about this section of the annual return so that you are not tempted to include expenditure which stands no chance at all of being allowed. A word with the tax office before you complete the return could save time and correspondence.

INTEREST ON LOANS

We can deal with two sections together here because the above heading is encompassed by a series of conditions which may be conveniently regarded as applying generally. The significance of the date 27th March 1974, apart from being budget day, is that, from then onwards, tax relief has been somewhat limited, and is available only if the loan, by its nature, qualifies for it.

This is not the place to go into the lengthy details which now surround loan interest and tax relief. I am merely endeavouring to assist the ordinary person in the completion of a tax return. If you want to know all the ins and outs, you should obtain the free Inland Revenue booklet IR11.

Having disposed of generalities, let us see what would normally be found in these sections in a return from the ordinary person. First and foremost, I suggest the normal Building Society mortgage interest, followed closely by interest to a local authority for house purchase or improvements. These are qualifying loans for tax relief and the annual gross interest is reported by these bodies to the tax office. No need here, therefore, for anything but the name of the lender and the account number. They have thoughtfully drawn a line for you through the amount column. Turning now to banks, it is a cardinal rule that interest on an overdraft is no longer of any use for obtaining tax relief. If they can be so persuaded, however, banks do lend money. As long as a bank loan was used for the purchase of your only or main residence, or improvement to it, then it will qualify for tax relief up to a maximum of £25,000. To those whom it may concern, a certificate must be obtained from the bank and enclosed with the return. The amount of the interest to be shown in the return will be obtained from this certificate.

Property which is let at a commercial rent may be the subject of a loan for its purchase or improvement. The interest, with certain reservations, does rank for tax relief, but I do not visualize more than a fraction of the ordinary taxpaying public being interested in this subsection. Those who are will find full details on page 8 of the booklet IR11.

At this stage, I will repeat that interest on loans incurred before 27th March 1974 was not subject to such stringent conditions as now. Interest incurred on earlier loans (not overdraft interest), although *not necessarily incurred for house purchase or improve-*

ment, is available for tax relief until 5th April 1980. Those concerned should therefore obtain a certificate for any other loan incurred before 27th March 1974 and insert the appropriate amount in the last subsection of the second section.

ALTERATIONS IN UNTAXED INCOME OR OUTGOINGS

Untaxed income

You will notice here that it is untaxed income which is singled out for a note of any alterations since the completion of the previous return. There are two reasons for this. In the first place, the notice of coding for 1978/79 will almost certainly have been issued before the tax office has a note of your 1977/78 untaxed income. This will probably mean that any deduction from allowances in the notice of coding will have been based on your untaxed income of 1976/77. Thus, a note of any increase or decrease in the current return will enable the tax office to adjust the 1978/79 code number if necessary.

Secondly, where, in certain circumstances, Schedule D assessments are raised separately on untaxed income, a note of any alteration in the amount received in 1977/78 will give the tax office the opportunity of revising the 1978/79 Schedule D assessment which would probably have been issued in October 1978, or even earlier. You would have appealed against the original assessment on the grounds that it will not agree with the untaxed income when the return is lodged.

Having dealt with the reason for the inclusion of this section in the annual return, I should perhaps refer briefly to such untaxed income as would normally be found there. War $3\frac{1}{2}\%$ loan and other government securities, the interest on which is paid gross, could figure prominently. You may have sold your holding or made a new investment. Details of sales and purchases should be clearly indicated—on plain paper if there is no room in the section itself.

Bank deposit interest is another item of untaxed interest which can fluctuate considerably. If, during the tax year, you have placed substantial amounts on deposit, or made sizeable withdrawals, the interest for 1977/78 could be very different from that of 1976/77—on which the tax office may have based an original notice of coding or assessment under Schedule D. Here again, give full details if necessary under this section.

Outgoings

The sudden appearance of an outgoing in an annual return may lead the tax office to think that perhaps a covenant payment or alimony, for example, has been paid for an earlier year or years, and has been overlooked by the taxpayer in previous returns. The earlier omission of a qualifying loan could lead, in due course, to a refund of tax. This is the place, therefore, in which to advise the tax office of details of a newly-effected covenant, mortgage, or whatever, and to mention, particularly, the commencing date.

CAPITAL GAINS

Whether you have disposed of chargeable assets, or acquired new ones during the year for which the return is being made, in my experience it is almost always the case that a separate statement is necessary. Here again, I have dealt with this in the chapter on the preparation of various statements which accompany returns.

In any case, and whether or not you have room in the return itself, it is very useful indeed to have a copy of capital transactions. It makes it very much easier for you to keep track of part disposals, and the acquisition of further shares in companies where shares are already held. It also enables the tax office to agree the individual gains and losses, and thus the net gain or loss for the year which will have been carried from the statement to the return in the shape of one figure.

The taxation of development gains is something so complicated in its provisions and, indeed, so remote in the possibility of its affecting the ordinary taxpayer, that there is nothing to be gained by any suggestion here regarding an entry in the annual return.

2

PREPARING STATEMENTS TO ACCOMPANY ANNUAL RETURNS

I have already referred, in the chapter on the completion of the annual return, to the very small amount of room provided for details of certain income. In a large number of cases the answer, of course, is a separate statement on plain paper, and one figure in the return labelled 'see statement attached'.

I have always given considerable importance to the presentation of a statement for the tax authorities. Over the years I have had ample proof of this by the fact that I have invariably received rapid agreement to accounts as presented. This has saved a great deal of time on both sides. I have a feeling that a return lodged soon after the 5th April, backed up by clear and concise statements where necessary, will be early in the queue for attention.

Not everyone, of course, has a typewriter. If you have, and can use it to good effect, a typed statement will carry a lot of weight, and you have a copy for immediate use in any subsequent correspondence with the tax office. Failing this, it has to be handwritten, but a carbon copy may still be taken. If you give yourself plenty of room on a large sheet or sheets of paper, the result could nearly match the typewritten one. From long experience, however, I would suggest that even a badly typed statement from an inferior machine has the edge over a handwritten one which is difficult to read.

Investment income

Let us assume that John Smith is preparing his 1978/79 income tax return. That is to say, he is submitting a return of his income from all sources arising in the year ended 5th April 1978. Both he and his wife have various investments and money in Building Societies. His first task will be to gather together all the counterfoils which should have been safely stored in a large envelope with his tax file. He will separate his wife's from his own, and then further separate the holdings of each into:

1. Dividends with tax credits
2. Interest taxed at source
3. Untaxed interest
4. Building Societies

Three further points before he starts. It is a good idea to put all the vouchers into alphabetical order. In a long list, a particular dividend may then be readily found. Another good idea to shorten the list is to add together two dividends or amounts of interest received in the same year, and show one total. This is quite acceptable. Finally, it is the date of payment of a dividend which decides the tax year in which it should be included—not the period for which the dividend is paid.

This is the statement which accompanied John Smith's return:

John Smith   *Investment income 1977/78*

Dividends with tax credits

Self	Source	Dividend £	Tax credit (34%) £
400	A.V.P. Industries ordy.	10·40	5·36
300	Distillers ordy.	19·31	9·95
350	I.C.I. ordy.	51·73	26·64
1234	Nat. Westr. Bank ordy.	68·68	35·38
200	Union International 6% pref.	8·40	4·33
		£158·52	£81·66

Wife	Source	Dividend	Tax credit
£500	Tube Investments ordy.	89·27	45·99
700	I.C.I. ordy.	103·46	53·30
1345	Midland Bank ordy.	67·25	34·64
		£259·98	£133·93

Interest or dividends with tax deducted at source

Self	Source	Gross	Tax deducted
£191	Imperial Continental Gas 7% L/S	13·37	4·55
£2000	Treasury 9% 1992/96	180·00	61·20
		£193·37	£65·75

Wife

£4101	Treasury 9% 1992/96	369·09	125·49
£2050	Treasury 13¼% 1997	140·83	47·88
		£509·92	£173·37

Total income as above for tax purposes £1337·38

You have my assurance that if the details of your investment income are set out in this way it will be exactly the kind of statement your tax office is looking for. It will be observed that I have abbreviated as much as possible the details in the first column. This is perfectly acceptable if consistent with clarity. The total at the foot of the page is handy for quick reference when checking any investment income surcharge.

If there were further sources of unearned income, the second page of the statement might read like this:

John Smith   *Investment income 1977/78 (contd.)*
Untaxed income
Self

	£2000	War 3½% Loan	£ 70
	£1000	Conversion 3½%	£ 35
			£105

Wife

	£1000	British Savings Bonds	£ 85

Building Societies

Self	Halifax	£ 22·50
Wife	Guardian	£ 35·50

This is the extent to which a separate statement of income should go. Such items as bank deposit interest, TSB interest and National Savings Bank interest will go straight into the return itself.

Dividends etc., from abroad
I have already mentioned that overseas dividends are normally received through paying agents in this country. These agents are authorized to deduct UK tax, but they are also allowed to give the appropriate credit for any overseas tax which has been suffered.

Although the annual return incorporates a section for *untaxed* income from abroad, it is obviously not the section for any overseas dividends received through a paying agent.

Such dividends should therefore be included in the section for 'other dividends, etc., already taxed'. That is to say, they may be included in the statement of income which has been taxed at source as long as sufficient information is given whereby double taxation relief may be allowed as necessary.

For example, the following dividend could have been included with John Smith's interest or dividends with tax deducted at source:

Source		Gross	Tax deducted
International Nickel		£50	
10% Canadian tax	£5		
24% deducted by paying agents	£12		£17

Letting property

In the chapter on the completion of the annual return I indicated that I would give you more detailed instructions with regard to the letting of property when I dealt with the preparation of the various statements which accompany the return. Thus, before I show you the content of an acceptable statement of letting, I would regard it as helpful to discuss the various items which would normally satisfy the tax office, so that none should be overlooked.

Unfurnished letting

I imagine that this is the more common type of letting, and it does differ in some measure, as regards items of expenditure, from the furnished letting.

I always favour beginning with the credit side for the taxpayer. That is to say, the cash received from the tenant(s), or perhaps via agents, in the case of a number of properties owned by the same landlord. Having established the rent to which the landlord became entitled by reference to the tenancy agreement, it is not difficult to arrive at a figure of gross income for the year in the account.

The expression 'became entitled' is important because the amount of money to which one becomes legally entitled in any particular year may not—and often is not—the amount which he actually receives within that year.

I think it would be accepted that the usual quarter days are those on which the payment of rent normally becomes due. Lady Day, or 25th March, is the particular quarter for which the rent may not be received until after the following 5th April. Nonetheless, if the landlord became legally entitled to a quarter's rent on, say, 25th March 1979, this must appear as a receipt in his 1978/79 account, even though not received until, say, 30th April 1979. This is illustrated in my example.

It is a fact of life that anyone who lets an unfurnished property wants to be left with as much net income after tax as may be legally obtained. It is therefore important that all expenditure which is admissible for tax purposes be included in the outgoings side of the letting account.

Most of you will remember the maintenance claims which so many of us used to make against the Schedule A assessment on the notional rent which, in the open market, an owner-occupier would be expected to receive if the property had been let. Those bad old days have gone, thank goodness, but the expenditure which was accepted is virtually no different from that which is normally admitted against the rent from an unfurnished letting. That is to say, the well-tried and accepted formula of maintenance, repairs, insurance and management.

Maintenance

This will embrace the cost of protecting the property from dilapidation. Examples are replacement of rusted gutters, pointing of brickwork, re-washering taps, and replacing rotten woodwork, rusted windows and broken tiles. You name it—if it maintains the property in a condition necessary for the letting, it should be allowed.

Repairs

If these are due to deterioration within the period of the lease, the cost should be allowed. Examples would be repairs to drives which have become dangerous, to pipes which have rusted, to chimneys which are crumbling, and so on.

Insurance

Premiums on insurance against the risk of damage by fire, flood, etc., to the building only. Not, however, for insurance against loss of rent.

Management

Agents' commission, accountancy fees for statements of letting. Gardeners' wages. Ground rent. Tenancy agreement costs. Advertising.

In addition, expenditure on rates, heating, lighting, etc., for which you, as landlord, have undertaken, by agreement, to pay without reimbursement.

Here is an example of what I hope may be regarded as a typical account of the letting of an unfurnished house owned by the ordinary person in addition to the main residence.

David Jones
Account of letting of 20 Gower Road, Swansea for 1978/79

Outgoings		Receipts	
General & Water rates	£ 95	Rent £10 per week payable	
Painting garage doors	£ 18	on the usual quarter days	
Replacement of broken		3 quarters to 25.12.78	£390
fencing	£ 75		
Fire insurance on house	£ 16	Due 25.3.79 but received	
Replacing rusted gutters	£ 64	15.4.79	£130
New tenancy agreement	£ 15	Tenant's contribution	
Sundry small items	£ 13	towards the bill for	
Balance—being *profit*	£249	fencing replacement	£ 25
	£545		£545

An account presented in this manner shows clearly that the profit is a genuine £249. The Inspector of Taxes may, of course, ask for a sight of the tenancy agreement, but I have seldom known this to be required. In a bad year for the landlord, it may happen that allowable expenditure exceeds the entitlement to rent in the year. This will not often be the case, but a deficiency in any year may be carried forward and set against future rent from the same property.

Furnished letting

It may be that some of us are fortunate to inherit a furnished property (don't look at me—that I should be so lucky!). Alternatively, there are some who can afford to purchase as an investment a seaside bungalow or a country cottage, and to furnish it for letting. The allowable outgoings are not very different from those attributable to an unfurnished letting—but there *are* differences.

The main difference stems from the fact that you own the furniture and other items which attract tenants who are looking for a home from home in which to spend a holiday away from it all. Thus, an insurance premium covering house *and* contents will be allowed. Wear and tear of furniture also comes into the reckoning.

The following is an example of a furnished letting. This relates to a furnished seaside bungalow owned by the taxpayer, used by him and his family during school holidays, and let during the time when they are not in occupation.

James Robinson
Account of furnished letting of 'Dormers', Runton Road, Cromer, for the year ended 5 April 1979

Outgoings		Receipts	
Agent's commission	£26	Rent	
Advertising	£ 8	8 wks May/June 1978 @	
Replacement of crockery, linen, etc.	£22	£21/wk	£168
		8 wks Sept/Oct 1978 @	
Wear and tear of furniture 10% of (£414-½ of £58)	£38·50	£20/wk	£160
Gardener's wages for the summer months £60—4/5ths claimed	£48	Odd winter lettings 5 @ £10/wk	£ 50
		2 wks March 1979 @ £18/wk	£ 36
		23 weeks	
23/52nds of the following:			
General & Water Rates £ 58			
Insurance £ 15			
Repairs to roof & gutters £ 47			
£120			
£120 × 23/52=	£ 53		
Balance—being profit	£218·50		
	£414		£414

Self-employment and freelance work

The accountancy profession will tell you that you would normally expect to find a balance sheet with a profit and loss account. Maybe so, but I am dealing here with the ordinary person's statement for the tax office, to show them, in a simple way, how he arrives at the net profit for the year which appears in his annual return.

With companies and the larger businesses it is, of course, a different matter. A balance sheet is the normal accompaniment to a trading account by reference to established accountancy principles. You will know, however, that I am not concerned here with the kind of statements which accountants prepare for companies and larger businesses. I deal with the smaller part-time professional and business accounts, and may the Inland Revenue forgive me if I say that I have never yet submitted a balance sheet. An occasional agreement with the bank statement, yes, but otherwise nothing more than a clear statement of receipts and outgoings leading to a usually readily-agreed figure of net profit.

Receipts

These must be made up of:

1. Actual cash received within the tax year concerned.
2. The cash expected for work completed within the year but not received before the year's end.

Outgoings

On this side of the account you should show every item of expenditure which has been laid out wholly and exclusively for the purpose of the trade or profession.

Obviously, I cannot cover by example every trade, profession, spare-time work and so on. I have therefore made the example below as comprehensive as possible in order that you may understand the kind of layout which, in my experience, appears to find favour with tax offices, and leads to their agreement without the bother of subsequent correspondence. The example therefore covers full-time self-employment because this embraces a wide selection of items making up such a statement. The principles covering part-time work are the same, but possibly on a smaller scale regarding details.

William Sparkes
Account of electrical and radio repair business for the year ended 5th April 1979

Outgoings			Receipts	
Wages to wife for dealing with telephone calls and for typing accounts and reminders—£5 per week		£260	Cash received during the year	£2748
Renewal of out-of-date equipment for testing circuits		£135	Cash due for work carried out within the year but not yet paid for	£ 162
Renewal of special technical tools		£ 86		
Telephone				
Total a/c for year	£120			
Proportion for business 2/3rds as agreed		£ 80		
Travelling				
Van used wholly & exclusively in the business				
Tax	£ 40			
Insurance	£ 57			
Petrol & oil	£125			
Servicing	£ 62			
		£284		
1 room in house used wholly and exclusively as a radio workshop				
Rates	£156			
Heating	£180			
Lighting	£ 64			
	£400			
1/6th claimed as agreed		£ 67		
Postage		£ 20		
Stationery		£ 11		
Net profit		£1967		
		£2910		£2910

Notes

1. The £260 wages to wife must not be overlooked when completing the relevant annual return. They should appear in the section for earnings from employment—the employer being William Sparkes.

2. *Renewal* of tools and equipment is admissible expenditure. The purchase of new or secondhand plant will rank for capital allowances, and expenditure on it is not an admissible outgoing in the trading account. A statement of capital allowances will be found later on.

3. A room in one's dwellinghouse used wholly and exclusively in the

business or profession obviously attracts a proportion of the rates, etc., on the whole property. The allowable business proportion is normally represented by the fraction one room over the total number of main rooms in the house—usually somewhere between one fifth and one seventh. Once the fraction has been agreed with the Inland Revenue, it is normally static for that particular house.

4. The telephone expenditure for business purposes is also a matter for negotiation with the tax office. It hinges largely upon the particular circumstances. Living, as I do, some considerable distance from London—not to mention Cardiff, Manchester, and so on, where the Inland Revenue is substantially decentralized—a fair and reasonable 5/7ths of my total telephone account is allowed.

The above is an example of a person's sole livelihood from self-employment. I think, however, that it might be helpful if I also refer to the situation where a safe employment provides the bread-and-butter, and a reasonably profitable sideline the jam. There are a few special points about this situation.

In the first place, an account, for tax purposes, of what may be termed profitable spare-time work may be quite a simple statement as long as it is clear and acceptable to the tax office. It may, of course, be accepted only after negotiation. One or two items of expenditure could possibly be the subject of reasonable and legitimate enquiry by the Inspector. This should not frighten the ordinary taxpayer who is doing his best. It will hopefully guide him towards a format leading to acceptable accounts in the future.

Before we go any further, I think there has to be a searching of consciences as to whether a particular activity should, for tax purposes, be regarded merely as a hobby or as a business. Perhaps I may endeavour to put those consciences into perspective. From the occasional sale, a hobby may, admittedly, attract the odd amount of cash, but, overall, it may be nowhere near a business in the accepted sense for tax purposes.

As you would expect, there have been many cases in the Courts covering this grey area. Broadly speaking, it may be said that even if one's leisure activity in a certain direction—be it photography, metalwork, pottery, or whatever—leads to a receipt of cash, the cash received may still not be any more than the necessary outlay. In other words, it may still be regarded as a hobby from which the odd amount of money received should not, in equity, be liable to tax.

Where, you may well ask, do you draw the line between what

should be included in the annual tax return and that which may, with a quiescent conscience, be swept under the carpet? In my opinion, it is really only the taxpayer himself who can answer this.

My own recipe, for what it is worth, is this. A hobby leading to a very occasional sale—no reference to it in the annual tax return. A hobby which is fast developing into a regular business—a reference to it in the first annual tax return after one realizes that it is becoming something of an attraction for regular annual income.

For example, Frank Ashton retired at 60 after 40 years in employment. He had always been interested in watercolour painting and, during his working life, regarded this as his major hobby. He became very proficient at it, and word got around about this proficiency soon after he retired to the West Country.

He was, in fact, persuaded to mount a small exhibition at one of the local public houses. The result was startling—but most rewarding. All but one or two of the pictures were sold within a few days, and he was besieged for many more paintings of scenes which the local inhabitants cherished.

In retirement, Frank found himself working at his painting almost full-time. He realized that he was making an additional income which augmented his moderate pension to a pleasant extent. In other words, he realized that he was engaging in part-time work which would bring him in an income for many years to come, and he must report it in his annual income tax return.

It was, however, costing Frank quite a bit to do these paintings, although they were selling very well. This is the crunch. A tax-payer must be fair to himself as well as reporting the extent of income from any particular source to the Inland Revenue to the best of his knowledge and belief. He is entitled, via tax law, to set against income any expenditure incurred wholly and ex-clusively in the course of a business or profession.

Sensibly, Frank gave this some thought. He decided that there definitely were items of expenditure wholly and exclusively incurred for the purpose of his painting. He came up with the cost of materials, framing (he sold the pictures already framed), one bedroom used exclusively as a studio, and car expenses for journeys made exclusively in connection with this work. He kept a record of this last item in a little book. The following was his account for 1977/78 which was agreed without question by his Inspector of Taxes.

Mr Frank Ashton
Account of watercolour painting for year to
5th April 1977

Outgoings			Receipts for sales	£764
Artist's materials		£ 63	Picture completed but	
Framing—42 pictures at £4 each		£168	not yet paid for	£ 18
Car expenses on journeys to painting sites:				
Mileage				
Total for year	6200			
Total for painting	1400			
Total car expenses	£330			
Allow 1400 =		£75		
6200				
1 room used exclusively for painting:				
Total rates, heating & lighting	£418			
Allow 1/6th		£ 70		
NET PROFIT		£406		
		£782		£782

Capital transactions

Simplicity is the keynote where capital transactions are concerned. The tax office can check budget day values, details of takeovers and your arithmetic. The material for your statement will come from contract notes and from previous years' statements in your tax file. The following example shows the simple format which I have adopted for some years. I have rarely had a comeback unless my arithmetic has let me down.

Mr Ian Vesta
Capital Transactions 1977/78

BP Ordy.			
106 acquired 1969/71	for		£623
106 sold 17.9.77	for		£619
		LOSS	£ 4

Courtaulds ordy.

650 acquired 2.11.72	for		£1177
650 sold 17.9.77	for		£ 708
		LOSS	£ 469

Shell T. & T. Ordy.

500 acquired before 6.4.65 BDV £1·63=cost of £825 (actual cost £715)

270 sold 17.9.77	for		£1032
deemed BDV of 270 shs =			
270 × £825	=		£445
500		GAIN	£587

Slater Walker High Income Trust

1300 acquired 1.6.71	for		£495
1300 sold 17.9.77	for		£264
		LOSS	£231

SUMMARY

Gains		£587
Losses		£704
	NET LOSS	£117
Less Loss c/fwd. from 1974/75		£232
Loss to carry forward		£349

The above example is obviously concerned only with sales. The annual return, however, also calls for acquisitions. Here again, the accompanying statement should be simple and concise. The following example is in a form which both satisfies the tax office and constitutes a ready reference in one's file for the preparation of a statement of gains or losses in the future.

Mr Ian Vesta

CAPITAL TRANSACTIONS 1977/78

11th February 1978
    Sold £300 Treasury 9% Loan 1992/96 for £210
    EXEMPT—held for more than 12 months.

1st April 1978
    42 De la Rue New Ordy. Shs. NIL PAID.
    Sold for £12. As the proceeds of this part-disposal are small, it is suggested that the £12 be deducted from the original cost (see below).

ACQUISITIONS

Self
22nd December 1977

300 BSR Ordy. for	£480
Less proceeds of rights	£ 12
	£468

900 Coats Patons Ordy. for	£478
400 Commercial Union Assurance Ordy. for	£358

Wife
20th September 1977
£2050 Treasury 13¼% 1997 for £1850

Capital allowances

One may reasonably assume that the majority of capital allow-ances statements are prepared by accountants and taxation practitioners on behalf of their taxpaying clients. The ordinary taxpayer will thus require merely a basically simple statement which is readily acceptable to the tax office. The following is an example of the kind of statement which appears to satisfy them.

Mrs. Gowin-Storrs   Freelance Market Researcher

Capital Allowances 1977/78

Motor Car Ford Capri PVC 456M

Balance 5.4.77		£829
Mileage incurred in work		
Hull—3 times	1020 miles	
Worthing—once	100 ”	
Liverpool—once	300 ”	
Various short journeys	240 ”	
	1660	

Total mileage 76/77—8600	
Writing-down allowance 77/78—25%	£207
Balance 5.4.78	£622
Allowance claimed 1977/78:	
$\frac{1660}{8600} \times £207$	£ 40

Desk & Bookcase

Balance 5.4.77	£10
Writing-down allowance—25%	£ 3
Balance 5.4.78	£ 7

Typewriter

Purchased 21.2.77 for	£70
First-year allowance claimed	£70

Total allowances claimed 1977/78—£113

On the purchase of new equipment, except for motor vehicles used other than for hire purposes, the taxpayer is entitled to a First-year allowance equal to 100% of the cost of the asset. If he wishes, he may disclaim this allowance and use instead the 25% writing-down allowance. This option might be useful in a year in which his income is insufficient to absorb the full allowance.

Sales

The proceeds of sales of the capital item should be deducted from the 'pool' value of any capital items not fully written off and if the 'pool' value is insufficient to make the deduction, the surplus will give rise to a balancing charge. This should be recorded in the annual return under the heading 'Trade, Profession or Vocation'.

When the trading activity is permanently discontinued, the open market value of all of the assets then remaining, usually the proceeds of sale, should be deducted from the 'pool' value. Any surplus 'pool' value remaining will give rise to a balancing allowance in favour of the taxpayer. A shortage of 'pool' value will give rise to a balancing charge as above.

Exceptionally, a motor car should be treated as a separate 'pool' of expenditure for this purpose giving rise to balancing allowances or balancing charges on the occasion of each sale. Mileage is the basis of apportionment with regard to a motor car used for pleasure as well as business so the full writing-down allowance must be deducted so as to leave the true balance to carry forward to the next year. However, the appropriate restriction should be applied to any balancing charge or balancing allowance.

The capital allowances are usually calculated for a year ahead of the year's income recorded in the accompanying return. This is because the allowances must correspond to the assessment which is based on the previous year's income.

3

COMPLETING AN INCOME TAX CLAIM

General principles

The claim form which I shall deal with is the normal Inland Revenue form R40 which is used for an annual claim for a refund of tax. In particular, I shall refer to the R40 (1978) which applies to a claim for the year ended 5th April 1979. Before we get down to detail, I think it would be helpful to discuss the general principle which leads to the existence of a claim.

In my view, the claim which is the most easily understood is the one made by someone whose sole income is derived from investment income taxed at source and/or dividends with tax credits. The principle here is that at least the single personal allowance is due to every individual, whatever his or her circumstances.

To put it another way, *nobody's whole income should ever be taxed*. It follows—and I hope you do, too—that where tax has been suffered on the whole of the income there must be some of it to come back to the recipient of the income. Here is the simplest possible example to illustrate this:

1978/79 Single person under 65

Total income all from investments		Tax deducted
£1900		£627
Less personal allowance	£ 985	
Taxable income	£ 915	

Tax to pay on first £750 @ 25%		£187·50
on next £165 @ 33%		£ 54·45
		£241·95
Excess tax suffered and reclaimable		£385·05

Here we have a simple example of a claim for a refund of £385·05. In effect, it is a claim for basic rate tax on the single personal allowance. £985 at 33 % is £325·05 plus the benefit of the reduced rate of 25 % that is £750 at 8 % = £60.

This example is too simple, you may say. The single person would most likely be earning in order to supplement the £1900 investment income, which would not go very far these days. Fair comment. I hope you follow me if I point out that any earned income over £985 will be taxable. In other words, the whole of the personal allowance and reduced rates will have been used up against the first £1735 of the earnings and any further income—earned or unearned—must be taxed at the basic 33 %. The investment income has been so taxed, and the taxable part of the earnings will be dealt with by PAYE. Here it is in figures:

1978/79 Single person under 65

Earned income	£2500	*Tax*
Unearned income	£1000	£330
	———	
	£3500	
Less personal allowance	£ 985	
	———	
Taxable income	£2515	
	———	

£750 @ 25%	£187·50	
£1765 @ 33%	£582·45	
	———	£769·95
Tax to pay		£439·95

Here we have a situation where part of the tax liability is accepted as having been liquidated by the tax suffered on the investment income. In a perfect world—and indeed in a perfect tax coding situation, PAYE will have been collecting £36·66 a month, thus allowing for the £330 credit on the investment income.

I hope I have made it clear that there *should* be no refund of tax in this situation. There *could* be, however, where the code number did not adequately reflect the tax suffered on the investment income by an appropriate adjustment in the notice of coding.

This leads us naturally into another reason for a claim for a refund of tax. That is to say, where, for one reason or another, too much tax has been collected by PAYE at the close of a fiscal year. For the past few years tax offices have been making repayments of overpaid PAYE tax at the end of the tax year without making a formal assessment. A repayment order is forwarded by the tax office with form R37A-2. On the back of this form there is a clear calculation leading up to the words 'payable order now issued for'. It is easier for the taxpayer to understand the reason for his repayment—and, in most cases, I would have thought, to check the amount repaid.

There is a situation in which an annual return leads to a claim. I did not refer to it in detail in the chapter on the completion of a return because the end product is really a claim for a refund, and the receipt, in due course, of the refund itself.

Let us assume that in 1978/79 a widow of 70 had the state pension of £950 and taxed investment income of £2500. She will show these figures in her return of income arising in the year ended 5th April 1979. The Inspector of Taxes knows from past returns that she will be entitled to a refund of tax for 1978/79 because her untaxed income (the pension) will not be as much as her age allowance.

Somewhere about halfway through the year 1978/79 the widow may receive from the tax office form R38 and a request that she may care to forward investment income vouchers for a gross sum of £1250. They will have made a calculation which indicates that this provisional block of vouchers will lead to the maximum refund of tax due for 1978/79. They will tell the widow this, and the calculation would be as follows:

Pension	£ 950		
Dividends	£1250	Tax deducted	£412·50
	£2200		
Less age allowance	£1300		
Taxable income to date	£ 900		
	750 @ 25%	£187·50	
	150 @ 33%	£ 49·50	
			£237·00
		Repayment due	£175·50

This procedure means that the widow has not had to wait until after the 5th April 1979 to obtain her refund, and the tax office has relieved the pressure on its claims department which builds up soon after the 5th April each year. No further refund is due because any income over and above the provisional £900 shown above has been correctly taxed at 33%.

Claim form R40 (1978)

This is the standard claim form which calls for income from all sources, capital transactions and outgoings. If that is the case, you may be wondering why the completion of an annual return is necessary. The answer is that where the taxpayer's circumstances lead to the completion of an annual R40, the tax authorities do not insist upon an annual return in addition. This is eminently satisfactory for the taxpayer whose income is uncomplicated, because the R40 has been simplified in recent years as much as possible—bearing in mind that it takes the place of the normal return.

By submitting form R40 (1978) the taxpayer would, hopefully, receive a refund of tax within a couple of weeks. I say hopefully because it must be borne in mind that as soon as maybe after the 5th April in each year tax offices receive, in varying degrees, a considerable number of such claims. Many elderly taxpayers are dependent upon their tax refunds to bring up their spendable income to subsistence level.

One imagines, for example, that the Worthing tax offices must be somewhat inundated with claims soon after April 5th—Worthing having, I understand, a population with the highest average age in the country. They are probably also concerned with many instalment claims, but these are discussed later on.

Unless you are submitting your first claim on R40, you don't have to ask for a claim form. You will find that a claim form for the following year will accompany your repayment order for the current year. It will be accompanied also by a Tax Claim Guide and a prepaid envelope.

If, however, you do find yourself in a position to make a claim where none has been made before, you will obviously contact your nearest tax office. For example, I knew an elderly lady, with only the state pension, whose brother-in-law decided to help her by means of an annual covenant payment. From the year of the first payment she was entitled to a refund of the tax which he deducted. She obtained form R40 and has been making an annual claim for some years.

So now we come to the actual completion of the claim form R40 (1977). The first words you notice on it are to the effect that this particular form should not be used before 6th April 1973. I mention this because I have indicated elsewhere that claims from

1971/72 onwards are valid if lodged by 5th April 1979. The reason for this note is that, with the introduction of tax credits with dividends from 1973/74 onwards, the ruling of the current form is not quite appropriate to any earlier year. The earlier claims may, of course, be made, but the appropriate forms should be obtained from the tax office.

Apart from the usual headings on the front page relating to name, address and so on, you will find an authority to pay the refund of tax to a banker, agent or other person. On earlier forms R40, one did not find this printed authority. I have by me an old R40 (1970) which did not include it. Some past forms also bore the message 'it is not necessary to employ an agent'.

Fair enough. It is not necessary, and you save money if you can formulate your own claim. You must, however, sign the declaration, and the authority is also there for your signature if you want to save yourself the trouble of writing out a separate one for the refund to go direct to your bank. Those who do employ an agent will find that he normally expects the authority to be signed in his favour so that he can check the refund and deduct his fee before remitting the balance to you.

As I have indicated, the main body of the claim beginning on page 2 may be regarded as a simplified version of the annual return. As taxed income, and/or dividends with tax credits, form the crux of almost every claim, they are, predictably, given the first two sections. You are given considerably more room here than is to be found in the annual return.

I still think that it is a good plan to make an alphabetical list of each on plain paper, with only the totals carried into the claim form plus 'see attached statement'. Can you distinguish between dividends with tax credits, and other income which has been taxed at source? It is not difficult.

Look carefully at your vouchers which will accompany the claim, and sort them into the two categories. Dividends with tax credits will have three columns as exemplified for 1977/78 by Shell Transport and Trading ordinary shares.

Number of shares	Tax credit	Dividend payable
1915	£66·86	£129·79

You will find that tax credits come with ordinary and preference shares, and ordinary stock.

Apart from the odd taxed annuity and covenanted payment, you will find that it is, in effect, *interest* vouchers which show *tax deducted* and *not* tax credits. That is to say, most government stock interest, debenture interest, and loan stock interest. Here is a typical example for 1977/78:

31st December 1977

Imperial Chemical Industries Ltd.
8% Unsecured Loan Stock 1988/93

Holding	Gross interest	Income tax @ 34%	Net interest
£4300	£172·00	£58·48	£113·52

The claim form, you will notice, does not call for the net income. It is not a bad idea, however, to make a total of the net income for yourself, so that you may check your other totals by subtracting the income tax deducted from the gross interest.

I have already suggested that the claim form R40 is used mostly by the more elderly taxpayers who have a measure of investment income to supplement the state pension. Widows, for example, whose husbands have left them a certain amount of capital, or single ladies who have been thrifty during their working life.

For this reason, I have explained the way to go about the completion of the investment income sections, although the preparation of statements in general has a chapter to itself. In other words, I have assumed that anyone looking for assistance in the completion of an annual claim would expect to find it all under one roof, as it were.

Having said this, I can see no valid reason for what would amount to almost complete duplication if I were now to deal with all the other sections of the R40 in detail. You will find, I hope, that the chapters on the completion of the annual return and the preparation of statements cover everything.

It only remains for me to say how much I deplore any kind of situation where money is left in the hands of the Inland Revenue which is not legally theirs. It is not their fault, mind you, and I have known of many instances where a tax office has pointed out to a taxpayer that a refund of tax may be obtained if an appropriate claim be lodged.

This is, naturally, a nice gesture and, in my view, goes a long way towards nailing the lie that the Inland Revenue is antagonistic towards the public. This is nonsense. I am, however, concerned for those elderly folk who may not, for one reason or another, have been made aware that money is due to them each year, and who are thus not claiming it. Many, alas, may be incapable of preparing a claim.

This may well be a situation which is becoming more prevalent. We are apparently all living longer—for better or for worse. Elderly folk who have managed to lodge claims for a number of years may well reach the point where they can no longer do so. What is the answer?

In many cases, of course, there are kindly relations, and possibly friends, who will take over the annual lodgment of a simple claim. There remains, however, the problem, in many cases, of obtaining the claimant's signature to the declaration on the R40. This is definitely a prerequisite to the admission and settlement of a claim by the tax authorities.

What, then, is the situation when an elderly person can no longer produce a signature acceptable to the tax office, or even produce a signature at all? The only way ahead, I am afraid, is for somebody to take out a power of attorney whereby he or she may sign the claim on behalf of the incapacitated person. A responsible person, normally a relative, will take this action via a solicitor, and may thereafter sign the declaration. The tax office will, of course, require a sight of the power of attorney, and will pay over any refund of tax to the holder of the power. It may well be that it will be paid over directly to a nursing home.

Instalment claims

I referred earlier to cases where the annual refund of tax is relied upon to maintain spendable income at a level which matches the essential annual requirement. This situation is anticipated by the Inland Revenue to the extent that they allow claims to be made more frequently than once a year. I knew a claimant who insisted upon and, in fact, obtained, a monthly settlement, but he was a crank who would have made a daily claim if he thought he had a chance.

Half-yearly and quarterly claims are the most usual, and these are, I would think, the most fair and reasonable intervals to both claimant and tax office. It must be remembered that a claim becomes possible only after a certain amount of taxed income has been received, and the total of dividends which come in during three months will, in most typical instalment claim cases, not amount to very much.

I would not wish an increase in work on Inland Revenue staff, but I do feel that there is a case for those with small incomes who are finding it a hardship to have to wait a whole year for a sum of money. They should be reminded that quarterly claims are possible. The following example illustrates the calculations in these cases.

1978/79	Widow of 70	
State pension	£950	
Dividends	£335⎫	£500 gross
Tax credits	£165⎭	

By 1st July our widow has received dividends amounting to £83·75, with tax credits of £41·25. She then completes an instalment claim for the period 6th April 1978 to 1st July 1978 and sends it to the Inland Revenue with the dividend vouchers. Shortly after this she should receive a repayment of the tax credits calculated as follows:

Pension	£ 950	
Dividends plus tax credits	£ 125	(Tax credit £41·25)
	£1075	
Age allowance	£1300	
Tax liability	NIL	

Payment of tax credits £41·25

You will probably have noticed here that a whole year's pension has been brought into the computation even at this early stage. It is essential to do this, otherwise there will be an over-repayment at some stage in the year. The whole untaxed income for the year must be incorporated at every stage.

By 1st October our widow has received another quarter's dividends of £100·50 (tax credit £49·50) and submits another instalment claim. The computation at this stage will be:

Pension	£ 950
Dividends plus tax credits received to date	£ 275 (tax credits £90·75)
	£1225
Age allowance	£1300
Tax liability	NIL
Tax credits to date	£ 90·75
Less already repaid	£ 41·25
Payment now due	£ 49·50

At the 1st January 1979, our widow has received another £60·30 (tax credit £29·70) and a further claim produces a repayment of £25·95 as follows:

Pension	£ 950
Dividends plus tax credits received to date	£ 365 (tax credits £120·45)
	£1315
Less age allowance	£1300
Taxable income	£ 15 @ 25% £ 3·75
	Tax credits to date £120·45
	£116·70
	Less already repaid £ 90·75
	Payment now due £ 25·95

In previous years as soon as our widow had used all her allowances no further repayment was due as the balance of her income would have been correctly taxed at the basic rate.

However, with the introduction of a reduced rate of 25% on the first £750 of taxable income a further repayment is due. We will now carry on and see what happens when our widow submits her claim for the final quarter to 5th April 1979.

State pension	£ 950	
Dividends plus tax credits	£ 500 (tax credits £165)	
	£1450	
Age allowance	£1300	
Tax liability	£ 150 @ 25%	£ 37·50
Tax credits		£165·00
	Balance due	£127·50
	Less already repaid	£116·70
	Repayment	£ 10·80

The one thing to remember is that you cannot always expect the same repayment in each quarter which is demonstrated by the repayments which our widow received in the previous example.

4

CHECKING AN ASSESSMENT

My aim, as I think you know, is to advise the ordinary taxpayer on such ordinary day-to-day problems as appear to me to arise. I thus endeavour to sort the wheat from the chaff by leaving the unusual one-off situation to the professional adviser who, one would assume, would be acting.

From the various Schedules, therefore, I shall deal with the two which relate to probably 99% of the assessments received by the ordinary taxpayer.

First, Schedule D, with its income from trades, businesses, freelance work, untaxed interest, foreign pensions, and so on. Secondly, Schedule E (form P70C) which assesses income from employment, ex-employers' pensions, family allowances, and frequently takes other odd sources of income under its PAYE umbrella.

Schedule D

There are subdivisions of this Schedule known as Cases, and income is assessed under a particular Case according to its source. The Case numbers do not appear on the notices of assessment. This is because a kind of universal Schedule D assessment form is used for all sources of untaxed income, and the various sources are labelled. I shall therefore discuss the checking of an assessment by reference to each source of income.

Earned income

I would not regard it as difficult to identify income regarded as earned for tax purposes. In any case, it happens to be singled out for special treatment in that the tax due on it may be paid by two instalments on 1st January and 1st July. Income from a trade, profession, consultancy work, and so on comes within this category.

You will find that the earned income always appears first under the Assessment Particulars. Except for the early and closing years (see below) you will find that the amount shown is—or should be —the net income shown in your trading account for the year before that to which the assessment relates. You have merely to look at your copy of the last return of income to check the figure. Your 1978/79 return, for example, which calls for income of 1977/78, provides the figure in your 1978/79 notice of assessment. You will need to apply special rules of assessment to check the figures when you have only recently begun part-time work, or whatever, and when you decide to finish with it.

First year of assessment

This will be the *actual* net profit from the date of commencement to the following 5th April. It is a good plan, if possible, to begin on the 6th April so that you get a whole year's net profit forming the basis of the first year's assessment. This saves an apportionment of net profits to get at the basis for the second year.

Second year of assessment

This will be the net profit covering twelve months from the date of commencement. If you started in, say, June 1977, the assessment for 1978/79 would be the profit in the 12 month period to June 1978.

Third and subsequent years

As I have indicated, the assessment now becomes based on the agreed net profits of the previous year. For those who did not commence actually on the 6th April the basis should be stated as the net profits shown by the annual trading account ended within the tax year preceding the year of the assessment being checked.

There is a proviso, however. If, by the way the net profits are going, it would be beneficial to the taxpayer, he may elect to have the assessments for both the second and third years subsequently adjusted to the actual profits of each of the two years. I mention this merely to round off the basis of assessment situation, but you may expect your third year's assessment to be based initially upon the profits of the previous year. If the election is made, revised assessments for the second and third years will arrive in due course and any refund which is due will be made.

Should any appeals be lodged? The answer is yes, only if either of the second and third year's assessments is an estimated one for any reason. For one's own protection, estimated assessments (where there is an 'E' against the amount assessed) should always be appealed against within 30 days from the date on the notice. This gives you time to lodge a belated annual return (if that is the trouble), or to point out to the tax office that the relevant return is in their hands, and that they should have been able to make an exact assessment first time.

Unless there happens to be an estimated assessment, you would normally only question, and thus appeal against, a second-year and/or a third-year assessment where it or they did not agree with the actual and previous year's profits respectively. You could not tell, until receiving the third-year assessment, whether it would benefit you to elect or not for a revision to the actual profits for both years. In any case you have to give notice in writing within 7 years of the end of the second year, and can revoke the election, if you wish, within 6 years of the end of the third. These applications may be regarded as taking the place of any appeal.

There is a source of income assessable under Schedule D which requires a special mention for purposes of checking it. I refer to a *pension* from *overseas*. From 1974/75 onwards, the assessment is on 90% of the full amount arising in the previous year. It is only 50% for certain German and Austrian pensions to victims of Nazi persecution and in some special cases may even be totally exempt from tax.

There may be one figure in the notice of assessment which covers two or more overseas pensions, and this figure may look a bit odd at first—particularly in a case where the tax office does not show any calculations.

I happen to have a good example of this. The taxpayer is retired, but was employed by both Shell Royal Dutch and the Netherlands Merchant Navy. Among the items in his 1978/79 Schedule D assessment is 'Dutch Pension £4442'. To check he must look back at his income for 1977/78 and he finds:

| Shell Royal Dutch pension from Holland | £4409 |
| Merchant Navy Pension from Holland | £ 527 |

He will find, therefore, that the two pensions for 1977/78 came to £4936, which, at 90%, is £4442·40. So he will be satisfied with the assessment on his overseas pensions.

Is that the extent of the sources of earned income which the taxpayer may expect to find in his Schedule D assessment? Not quite. He may have a wife who is qualified to engage in, say, consultancy work. If so, he may expect her net earnings by reference to a submitted account to appear below his. They should be the amount earned in the previous year.

UNEARNED UNTAXED INCOME

Here again, the items may be readily checked because they will normally be the income arising in the previous year. Items such as bank deposit interest, National Savings or TSB interest (the excess over £70 for both husband and wife), interest paid gross on certain Government holdings such as War $3\frac{1}{2}$% loan, and so on.

I must point out, however, that where, as is usual, the interest first arose after the 6th April in any year, the first two years' assessments will be based on the actual income arising in those two years. Even the third year may be so based if the taxpayer finds it to his advantage so to elect. All this makes checking the figures no more difficult as long as accurate copies of returns are kept.

The last and penultimate years of the source also come in for special treatment. The last year's interest is assessed by reference to the actual amount arising from the 6th April to the date of the disposal of the source.

As far as the penultimate year is concerned, the Inland Revenue are legally empowered to raise an additional assessment if it is found, in due course, that the income arising within the twelve months to the 5th April of that year was greater than the original assessment. The original assessment for the penultimate year will, at the time, have to be checked by reference to the previous year because the Inland Revenue will not know (and the taxpayer himself may not) that the source would cease during the next year.

One final matter under this heading. You will notice that there are two columns for the actual amounts of the various items of income, and that unearned untaxed income always appears in the second column. This may puzzle a number of people, but this is done because the tax on it is payable in full on the 1st January, and it has therefore to be separated from the earned income in the first column.

To collect the tax on the unearned income, the tax office may allocate a proportion of the net allowances to this source. This proportion will be equal to the unearned income itself, leaving two equal instalments to pay. This must be regarded as a small concession because, in effect, it allows the taxpayer to pay by two equal instalments, although a proportion of the tax would really be due in a lump sum on the 1st January. In some cases, however, you may find that the whole of the allowances have been deducted from the earned income. This, of course, leads to a larger first instalment of tax than the second.

This leaves only a 'Balancing Charge' (if any) to be assessed, but very few ordinary taxpayers will be concerned with it. The circumstances in which it arises have already been dealt with on page 39. Where there are Capital Allowances, they will appear under 'Deductions', and these can be checked from the statement which accompanied the relevant return.

DEDUCTIONS

Retirement annuity payments
A deduction for the above is mainly applicable to the self-employed taxpayer whose earned income is assessable under Schedule D. Those who are paying an annual premium which leads to an annuity on retirement will obviously know the amount of it. Furthermore, they will, let us hope, have made sure via a good insurance broker or the insurance company itself that the contract has Inland Revenue approval for the purpose of tax relief.

That being so, and for the purpose of checking any deduction given in the assessment, the limitations on premiums allowed to be deducted should be known. For 1978/79, one is allowed the lower of 15% of the net relevant earnings, or £3000. Broadly speaking, the net relevant earnings, for Schedule D purposes, consist of the income from the trade, profession, etc., less any deductions which, for purposes of ascertaining the total income, would diminish such earnings.

There is, however, a measure of relaxation in these limitations for those who were born in 1915 or earlier. The following table, applicable to 1978/79, shows how the limitations are gradually extended as the birthdates of taxpayers are projected backwards.

Year of birth	Lower of	—or—	Percentage of NRE
1914 or 1915	£3600		18%
1912 or 1913	£4200		21%
1910 or 1911	£4800		24%
1908 or 1909	£5400		27%
1907 or earlier	£6000		30%

Where the premium paid in any year exceeds the prescribed percentage of net relevant earnings of that year, the excess may be carried forward and treated as a qualifying premium for the following year. You cannot do this, however, where the excess payments are more than the prescribed monetary maximum.

Although I have not really gone into detail with regard to deductions allowed for retirement annuity premiums, I am hopeful that those who are paying them will be able to check the amount which the tax office has allowed. It should not be overlooked that the net relevant earnings will not normally be known by either the tax office or the taxpayer at the date of issue of the notice of assessment. It follows that unless you are reasonably confident that the deduction allowed will be found, in due course, to be correct, you should appeal against the assessment where you consider that it should be greater when your income for the year in question is known.

Losses

Those who handle their own income tax affairs will presumably have been keeping a note of the occasional loss which they, or possibly their wives, may have made in, say, part-time consultancy work. A loss may be claimed as a deduction against any other income in the year of assessment in which it is made, as long as the trade or profession is being conducted on a commercial basis with a view to the realization of profit.

The 1978 Finance Act introduced an extension of this relief to encourage the starting up of new businesses which cannot help trading at a loss during the start-up period. The losses, including any losses created by the claiming of capital allowances, during the first 4 years of operation can be carried back and claimed as a deduction against any other income in the 3 years immediately preceding the year in which the loss occurs. No relief is available for losses incurred before 6th April 1978 although businesses which commenced before that date might still claim eligible losses within the four year time limit occurring after that date.

Losses may also be brought forward from earlier years where tax relief has not already been granted on them. If there is a figure against 'Losses' which you cannot understand, you should have a word with your tax office within the 30 days allowed for appeal. They will explain it, and will let you know whether you may claim anything further by way of losses brought forward from earlier years if it would be beneficial to you.

Building Society—other loan interest

This is a deduction which will have been estimated by your tax office. You will have some idea from your copy of the previous year's tax return what the interest will be. Building Societies give the Inland Revenue approximate figures from their records, and if any Building Society interest shown on the notice of assessment makes reasonable sense, it may be accepted. A loan from, say, the bank, for house purchase or improvement may occasionally be static, in which case you will be expecting a definite figure as a deduction. In the case of a reducing loan, the estimated figure may or may not be acceptable. If the loan happened to be repaid during the previous year, you would obviously appeal in order to save an additional assessment later on.

ALLOWANCES

With the exception of housekeeper allowance, you will find that all the items under the above heading on a Schedule D notice of assessment have been discussed in the chapter on the checking of a notice of coding. Housekeeper allowance would only very rarely be claimed by those taxed under PAYE, and there are a couple of blank spaces if it should apply. The claim situation where a housekeeper is employed is explained in the notes which come with the annual income tax return. The current allowance is £100 and from 1978/79 you can claim for a male housekeeper as well as for a female one.

This brings us to a possible further deduction from the total of allowances with the subheading of 'less allowed in Part III'. This is obviously something which needs explaining if you are to be able to check any figure which may be found here.

Part III at the foot of a Schedule D notice of assessment has two functions:

1. It collects tax on a source or sources of income which would otherwise have to be the subject of a separate assessment—probably under a different Schedule.

2. In cases where tax is payable at the higher rates, it separates, for arithmetical checking purposes, the ascending 'bands' of higher rate tax. This allows in Part II a lump sum and its appropriate tax, together with the odd income at the highest rate. In short, it keeps a clutter of detailed figure-work out of Part II.

In regard to (1) above, I have mentioned in the chapter dealing with coding notices that income can be effectively taxed by absorbing it by part of the personal, etc., allowances. Part III does just this, and the total of the allowances so absorbed should be carried to Part II, and should deplete the total allowances—leading to 'Balance given in this assessment'.

As well as checking the addition in Part III, you should also be in a position to verify the figure against a particular source of income, or even, in the light of your own information, say whether it should be there at all, a note should be kept of the amount of any state pension received to compare with the figures used in Part III. Untaxed income should be accurate, too, because the basis is the income of the previous year, and the amount would normally be known by the tax office at the date of issue of the notice of assessment.

I think an explanation of the workings of (2) above is best illustrated by an example. If we assume that the amount chargeable to tax in a 1978/79 Schedule D notice of assessment is £10,350, the following tabulation should be found in Part III:

Income charged at

40%	45%	50%
£1000	£1000	£350

Then, if we look over at Part II, we would expect to find:

Reduced rate	@ 25% on £ 750	£ 187·50
Basic rate	@ 33% on £7250	£2392·50
Higher rates	@ 40% on £1000	£ 400
	@ 45% on £1000	£ 450
	@ 50% on £ 350	£ 119

Before we arrive at the net tax payable, you will notice spaces allotted to an addition for investment income surcharge, and a deduction for life insurance relief. Now the precise surcharge for the year in question may not be known at the date of issue of the assessment notice. Therefore if it would be an estimated figure, you should appeal against it if you have reason to believe it will be far out for the year of the assessment.

The deduction for life insurance relief should be accurate by reference to the information in the hands of the tax office gained from your latest income tax return. Where, however, it happens to be wide of the mark as a result of additional insurance effected, or the maturity of an endowment policy, an appeal should be lodged.

However, the deduction for life assurance will disappear from 1979/80 onwards and tax relief will be obtained by a reduction in your payments to the Life Assurance Company.

Class 4 National insurance contributions
This recently-contrived controversial addition to the latest Schedule D notices of assessment is readily checked. It is levied only in relation to earned income, and the contribution for 1978/79 is 5% of the net profits between £2000 and £6250. It is payable in two instalments on the 1st January and 1st July, and half the amount for the year is added to each instalment of the tax on the net profits.

Appeals
I am hopeful that, having read and digested my analysis of a Schedule D assessment, the taxpayer who deals with his own

affairs will either be satisfied with it, or will have the confidence to appeal against it, knowing that he has genuine grounds for so doing. I should perhaps mention here that where a professional taxation adviser is employed, the latter will normally have lodged an authority whereby he receives copies of all assessments. In these cases, the taxpayer should have no need to forward the notice of assessment to his adviser. The latter will appeal where necessary.

Where the taxpayer is doing his own work, and regards an appeal as necessary, it must be made within 30 days from the date on the notice. A form of appeal would normally have been received with the assessment, and its completion is not difficult by reference to the explanatory notes which accompany it. Don't forget to complete Part 2 where it is considered that payment of part, or even all, of the tax should be postponed until agreement has been reached with the Inspector of Taxes.

5

CHECKING A NOTICE OF CODING

Those who are in employment, or who receive a pension from ex-employers, will know that the appropriate tax is deducted weekly or monthly from the earnings or pension. The PAYE system is, of course, the basis of this pseudo-painless extraction of tax.

In order that as accurate a deduction of tax as possible may be achieved, a code number is applied by the employer or ex-employer to pre-calculated tax tables supplied by the tax office. Since these tax tables are static, it means that the code number which applies personally to each and every taxpayer according to his or her circumstances is of vital importance to the correct tax deduction.

It follows, of course, that the material from which the code number is calculated needs to be as accurate as is humanly possible. It stems, in fact, from the taxpayer's latest annual income tax return—the importance of which is stressed in another chapter. The number, in its final form, is, in fact, the first two figures of the taxpayer's net allowances. This is the figure which should be checked.

The only way to check one's code number is to make sure that the intermediate figures leading up to it are themselves correct. To this end, we must go through the items on the notice of coding one by one. This is the blue-printed form P2 which is sent out to all employees and pensioners round about the February or March before the beginning of the tax year concerned. Some may be as late as May but, whenever received, it should be checked immediately.

Expenses, etc.
This item is the deduction from earnings normally allowed by the tax inspector for expenditure wholly, exclusively and necessarily

incurred in the performance of the duties of the employment. If, as is wise, you have kept a copy of past annual returns, you will know what you have been claiming. The usual items are travelling (but not between home and place of work), professional subscriptions, accepted round-sum expenses in certain employments, approved annuity contributions, and so on.

Building society interest payable
The normal situation here is that monthly payments consist of a combination of principal repayment and interest. As a result, the annual interest decreases year by year, and the Building Societies advise the appropriate tax offices of the interest expected from each borrower for the coming tax year. The figure in the coding may therefore be accepted as reasonably accurate unless the taxpayer knows definitely that it is a long way out. He may, perhaps, have paid off a substantial slice of capital late in the year and thus put a spanner in the liaison between tax office and Building Society. In that event, I would suggest that the Building Society be contacted in order that an underpayment of tax may be avoided by the issue of a revised notice of coding.

Loan, etc. interest
Let us consider what will appear under this heading. This will almost always be interest paid to a *bank* on a loan obtained for the purchase of a house or for the improvement of a house already owned. The yearly amount of interest may very occasionally be static but in the normal way the bank requires the loan to be repaid within a certain time. The interest would thus decrease year by year, as with a Building Society.

Checking the interest paid to a bank which appears in your coding notice is quite simple in the end but the tax office will, in most cases, have to estimate the amount of interest to be paid because the coding notice will have been prepared before the receipt of the annual return which reports it.

For example, in 1977/78 you may have paid gross bank interest of £80 on a loan granted for an extension to your house. Tax relief for 1977/78 was duly given on the strength of what appeared in the 'Outgoings' section of your annual return for that year. In February 1978, however, when the tax office sent out your 1978/79 notice of coding, they will only be able to estimate the interest payable. Depending on what they happened to know about the nature of the loan, they may repeat the figure of £80 or they may estimate it at, say, £60.

Now you hardly need me to tell you that you cannot expect in February 1978 a bank certificate for the loan interest which you will have paid for the tax year ending 5th April 1979. The question is, therefore, do you regard £60 as being a reasonably accurate estimate of the interest you are expecting to pay in the year ended 5th April 1979? This happens to be one of those grey areas which leaves the ball in the taxpayer's court. If, from the way in which you are repaying the capital, you are reasonably certain that your interest for 1978/79 is going to be far less than £60, tell your tax office immediately that you estimate it at, say, £20, and they will send you a revised notice of coding—probably in time for the beginning of 1978/79. After all, they will be as anxious as you to avoid an underpayment of tax at the 5th April 1978.

Personal allowance

By the time this book comes out there will almost certainly be alterations to the personal and other allowances by the 1979 Budget proposals. Although these are indicated in the Appendix, I must at this stage work on the 1978/79 allowances as confirmed by the 1978 Finance Act. If you are a single person under 65 your allowance should be shown as £985. If married, it should be £1535.

Age allowance

For those over 65 at some point within the tax year (either husband or wife where married), there is an age allowance which is more than the normal personal allowance. It is given in full as long as the total income is not more than £4000. For a married man it is £2075, and for a single person £1300.

In the notice of coding you will find the words '(estimated total income £......)' after the heading 'Age'. This is a safety measure to ensure as far as possible that an underpayment of tax does not occur at the 5th April. From past returns, the tax office has a fair idea of a taxpayer's total income, and the age allowance given in a coding will be scaled down where the income for 1978/79 is expected to be more than £4000. This is because the age allowance is reduced by two thirds of the excess over £4000 until the normal personal allowance is reached.

From what I have said you will realize that those over 65 whose total incomes exceed £4000 may expect to see a scaled-down age allowance in their notices of coding. This can be checked fairly accurately if you know more or less what your total income is going to be in 1978/79. Don't forget to deduct any charges on the income such as mortgage interest and so on.

The method is this. Reduce the age allowance by two thirds of the excess of total income over £4000. For example, a married man who estimates his total income for 1978/79 at £4300 will expect to find £1875 under age allowance in his coding notice. If the figure inserted by the tax office is very different from this, it might be possible to persuade the tax office that a revised coding should be issued.

For those with higher incomes there will come a time when the age allowance will be no more than the normal personal allowance. For a married man the normal personal allowance takes over at £4810, and for a single person at £4472·50. With higher incomes than these, one can expect only the personal allowance in the coding notice and nothing under 'Age'.

Wife's earned income

Only very rarely will there be a figure under this heading. This is because the allowance is normally given in the wife's coding for her employment or pension in her own right. If there is a figure for 1978/79, it will be £985, or the amount of her earnings or pension if less than £985.

Additional personal allowance

A claim here is the concern of those with only the single personal allowance, and married men with totally incapacitated wives who have single-handed responsibility for children living with them. The allowance for 1978/79 is £550.

Child allowance

For 1978/9 you will get relief for each of your children as follows:

Age on 6th April 1978	Allowance	Special
Under 11	£100	£300
11 or over but under 16	£135	£335
16 or over and full-time student	£165	£365

Because of the introduction of tax free child benefits, child allowances are now, in general, lower. If you do not receive child benefit for certain of your children, you might obtain child relief at the 1977/78 rates which were higher. This probably applies to certain older students and children living abroad for whom you are not eligible to claim child benefit.

For example, in October 1978, you had three children as follows:

> Child A born June 1968
> Child B born March 1964
> Child C born February 1961 and at school

For 1978/79 you would expect to find a total of £400 under the heading 'Children' in the 1978/79 notice of coding. If this were not the figure, the matter should be taken up with the tax office without delay.

You will have noticed the words 'including reduced allowance' against the child allowance section of the notice of coding. This is to allow a modification of the allowance where the child has a certain amount of income in its own right for the tax year concerned. To enable you to check a reduced allowance I should perhaps explain further.

The Finance Act 1976 made certain changes from the previous situation where the child allowance was reduced pound for pound by the amount by which the child's income exceeded £115, and was extinguished after the income had reached £115 plus the appropriate allowance. Where the child is under 18 on the 5th April 1979, and is not married by then, the £115 limit still applies to *unearned income* of the child. The good news for the parent is that a further £365 of *earned income* of the child will, in addition, not affect the parent's child allowance. In short, the 1978/79 child allowance will not be affected where the child's total income is £500, as long as £365 of it is earned.

The situation where the child is 18 or over, or is married at the 5th April 1979 is even better for the parent who is entitled to child allowance. The child's income—earned or unearned—may reach £500 before the child allowance is reduced pound for pound by the excess.

There are two other points to note. One, scholarship income or an educational grant is not income of the child for child allowance purposes. Two, the birth of a child during the tax year should be reported to the tax office without delay. A revised coding will be issued as long as the birth took place within a reasonable distance in time from the next 5th April. The tax office will decide about this, and if a revised coding is not appropriate there will normally be a refund of tax.

Dependent relatives
If there is an allowance under this heading it can be readily checked. You will know, from previous admission by your tax office, that you have been receiving an allowance for a dependent relative or relatives. If nothing has changed, you should expect to see £100 in respect of each relative whose income does not exceed the basic retirement pension. Any excess reduces the allowance pound for pound. Single women claimants would expect to see a maximum of £145—scaled down, if necessary, as I have indicated.

Life assurance
1978/79 is the last year for which you will have to check your deduction for life assurance. From 1979/80 onwards tax relief will be obtained by a reduction in the premium you pay over to the life assurance company.

However, for 1978/79, unless you were liable to pay higher rate of tax, the figure in your notice of coding would have been calculated as follows (subject to the restriction as indicated overleaf):

Total premiums	*Allowance in coding*
Under £10	Amount of premiums
£10 to £20	£10
Over £20	One half of the premiums

The restriction mentioned above is that relief is not given on more than one-sixth of the total income. Where, for example, the total income was £3000, total premiums of £600 would be scaled down to £500 (£3000 × 1/6) and one half, i.e. £250 would be the allowance appearing in the notice of coding. This restriction has to be calculated each year to take into account any increase, or decrease, in income.

The restriction will still apply in 1979/80 even though the method of giving relief has been radically altered but only where the total of qualifying premiums exceeds £1500. The new system assumes that almost everyone is entitled to relief at $17\frac{1}{2}$ % on all life assurance premiums paid but Insurance Companies are made responsible for deciding which policies qualify for the relief and which do not.

For those who were liable to pay higher rate tax in 1978/79, there was a special restriction for coding purposes only, if you estimated your highest rate you could then look in the PAYE coding guide under Life Assurance and this gives the fraction of allowable premiums to be given in the coding.

ALLOWANCES GIVEN AGAINST OTHER INCOME

Untaxed interest
This, and the next three subheadings, are inserted to save work in making separate assessments upon certain items of unearned income which has not been taxed at the source. In other words, the income can be effectively taxed by absorbing a proportion of the personal allowances equal to the income assessable.

Untaxed interest will embrace deposit interest from a bank, the excess, if any, over £70 for 1978/79 of National Savings or

Trustee Savings Bank interest, interest from Government Stocks paid gross, and so on. When checking this in your notice of coding remember two things:

1. Any National Savings or TSB interest assessable will be the amount received, less £70 for 1978/79, in the calendar year ended on the 31st December prior to the 5th April ending the tax year concerned.

2. Any other interest will normally be the amount which you received in the tax year preceding that to which the coding refers. Only in the first or last year or two will it be the actual interest of the tax year concerned. The previous year basis is useful for checking purposes because the amount will be known from the last annual return well before the notice of coding is received.

National insurance benefits

Here we have another deduction which saves making a separate assessment and ensures the collection of the appropriate tax by an increase in the monthly (or possibly weekly) PAYE deductions. When checking this it should be borne in mind that it may well be an estimated figure. This will depend upon the date on which the notice of coding is issued. We have become accustomed to April budgets in which there is a proposal to increase the state pension from the following November. Where the notice of coding has been sent out before the budget, the tax office would not be aware of any increase to come. In these cases a revised coding to take account of any increase in the state pension may be expected about June.

Whether the state pension figure is correct in the first place, or has subsequently to be revised, it is a simple matter to check it. You will know if it is provisional by the fact that it will be 52 times what you are getting when you receive the notice of coding. A revised figure will consist of so many weeks at the old figure and the balance of the year at the new.

For example, the various state pensions went up from November 1978. For 1978/79 this means 32 weeks at the old rate and 20 at the new. In terms of a married couple, where the wife has not been a contributor, you get a total for 1978/79 of £1520, and that is the figure, as originally shown or afterwards revised, which such a married man may expect to find. If it had been revised, PAYE will catch up with its deductions by the end of the tax year at 5th April 1979. The figure for single persons should be £950.

Those who find themselves qualifying for the state pension during a tax year should also have no problem in checking what appears in the notice of coding. A single person, for example, who became 60 on 3rd August 1978 would receive £17·50 a week for 15 weeks and £19·50 for 20. The pension for 1978/79 should be £652·50. Widows must remember the special widows' allowance for the first 26 weeks.

Occupational pensions

This subsection of deductible allowances caters, for example, for those who change their employment and are in receipt of a small pension from the previous employers' pension fund. It might also apply to a retired man whose previous firm's pension happened to be administered by a different tax district from that of the firm from which he finally retired. He will, in any case, know the amount of such a pension, and of any subsequent increases.

TAX UNPAID FOR EARLIER YEARS

Under the terms of the Income Tax (Employments) Regulations 1973 the Inspector of Taxes *may* require the amount underpaid for any earlier year to be paid over to the Collector of Taxes. Normally, however, this action will be taken only in the case of a substantial underpayment. Fortunately for the taxpayer, the majority of underpayments are deducted under the above heading from the net allowances in the next notice of coding.

If you find such a figure or figures in your notice of coding, it is not difficult to make a check. For 1978/79, for example, the deduction will be such an amount which, when taxed at the basic rate for the year of the coding, will leave the amount of the underpayment. If the latter is, say, £64, your deduction from the net allowances would be £193.

How do you know the amount of the underpayment? You may

ask. It will, in fact, appear in the penultimate space of your assessment on form P70C. For the previous year to that of the coding you will probably not yet have received a P70C, but for earlier years, you will. That is why the previous year is labelled 'estimated', but you can check it when the assessment does come in. The estimate made by the tax office will usually be pretty accurate because their records will show them more or less how the previous year's tax deductions have been going.

OTHER ADJUSTMENTS

You will find that items in this space are almost always used to collect the higher rate tax on dividends, taxed interest, or Building Society interest. This is something which, without help, the PAYE system cannot do. The tax office are obliged to estimate the 'band' of higher rate tax applicable to such income. Since it will already have suffered the basic rate ('notionally' in the case of Building Society interest), the adjustment gives PAYE a boost by adding a percentage to take it up to the highest estimated rate.

Bearing in mind that PAYE can deal with higher rate tax as well as basic rate, it has also to be remembered by those who fancy their arithmetic that although any adjustment in the coding whereby allowances are reduced will charge such adjustment to both basic and higher rate according to the amount of the earnings, the investment income, having already suffered basic tax, is to be taxed only at a certain percentage above the basic rate. This rather complicated business needs special tables for quick calculation—and your tax office has them. You may therefore rely upon such 'other adjustments' as you find in your coding notice.

GENERALLY

The final check is obviously the arithmetic. Historically, your tax office is good at this. In the course of long experience, however, I have found the odd mistake. Addition and subtraction in the hands of an over-worked tax office may very occasionally drift into an error of, say, £100. Don't bother about a few pounds. That will barely affect the code number, if at all, but an error leading to a substantial adjustment should naturally be pointed out.

6

THE HUSBAND AND WIFE SITUATION

There can hardly be a married man living who does not know that the income of a wife living with her husband is included in his total income for tax purposes. That is to say, he is legally responsible for the tax due on the aggregate of their two incomes where the wife has income of her own.

With that overriding principle established, it is necessary to qualify it by setting out the situations in which other factors may operate to change, in varying degrees, this basic rule.

'Living with her husband'

Tax law decrees that a married woman is regarded as living with her husband unless they are:

1. Separated under a Court Order or separation deed.
2. Separated in circumstances which render permanent separation likely.
3. Living together, as defined above, but one of them is resident in the UK for the relevant tax year, and the other is resident abroad.
4. Both resident, but one is absent abroad throughout the whole year. In that case, they are treated as permanently separated for that year, with two single personal allowances, provided that the aggregate tax bill is not thereby increased.

The year of marriage

1. The wife is assessed as a *single person* on the whole of her income for the year of marriage, unless the marriage took place on the 6th April.
2. The husband is entitled to the £1535 married personal

allowance. This is reduced, however, for each complete month from the 6th April to the date of marriage by 1/12th of the difference between the £1535 and the single personal allowance of £985. This is, of course, £550, and a wedding on, say, 15th October 1977, would give the husband £1260 for 1978/79.

Separate assessment
Although, as I have said, the husband is legally responsible for tax on the joint income of himself and his wife, *either spouse* may elect that they be separately assessed on every source of income received by them both. This is what I shall call normal separate assessment.

From 1972/73 onwards there has been allowed a kind of partial separate assessment. That is to say, an election may be made jointly whereby the wife's earned income is assessed on her as though she were a single person.

Normal separate assessment
Before we get down to detail, let it be said that normal separate assessment of the incomes of husband and wife does not affect the total tax payable. Why bother, then, when the checking of a separate assessment on each is quite a chore? It may not even be possible where strict secrecy over financial matters is the order of the domestic scene.

In my experience, a wife will normally elect for separate assessment in order that she may obtain a refund of tax in her own right by reference to the proportion of the married personal allowance which she is given, and her own taxed income. In other words, she rather objects to seeing the *whole* of her dividends eroded to the extent of 33 %.

A husband's election for separate assessment is, I think, equally valid. Where his wife's income is substantial, he is not normally enchanted by an inflated bill for higher rate tax and/or investment income surcharge. By electing, he can deflect a proportionate amount towards the bank account of the lady of his choice.

There may be a third reason—purely a domestic one. Perhaps neither husband nor wife wants the other half to know the extent and sources of his or her income. Since returns may be required from either party, or from both, a return from one or the other, which included only the income of the one who made the return, would force the hand of the Inland Revenue to ask the other spouse for a separate return. One assumes that domestic bliss would thereafter be resumed.

I indicated earlier on that the calculations necessary to arrive at an apportionment of tax between husband and wife on the strict basis by reference to tax law can be, and usually are, long and complicated. If I were to set out an example in figures, I doubt very much whether it would mean anything to the ordinary taxpayer.

The trouble is that there is so much more to it than might be imagined. The personal allowances have, for example, to be apportioned between the couple in the ratio of their income. Where higher rate tax and investment income surcharge come into the picture, you really get into deep water. Even if you do elect for normal separate assessment, I have my doubts that, as an ordinary person with no special knowledge of tax law, you would make anything of the apportionment calculations from the tax office.

However, here is a simple example for 1978/79, where both the husband's and wife's income is derived from employment.

		Total £ 10,000	Husband £ 6000	Wife £ 4000
Personal allowance	£1535			
Wife's earned income allowance	£ 985	2520	$\frac{8}{10}$ 1512	$\frac{4}{10}$ 1008
		7480	4488	2992
25% on £1500 =		375	187·50	187·50
22% on £5980 =		1973·40	1233·54	739·86
		(3738)	(2242)	
		2348·40	1421·04	927·36
			2348·40	

There is a point here which should be stressed. If separate assessment gives the wife less than the wife's earned income allowance due an adjustment has to be made whereby her allowance is brought up to this figure—at the expense of the husband. This would have happened in this example if the husband's income had been £6000 and his wife's only £2000. Her proportion of the personal allowances would have been ¼ of £2520, i.e. only £630 and would automatically have been increased to £985.

This example then demonstrates the method which the Revenue use to calculate the tax due when you elect for separate assessment, but it is important to bear in mind that the average family tax affairs are more complicated than this. There is usually a mortgage, life assurance, etc. and when the wife works or has a private income there could be the additional complication of higher rate tax and investment income surcharge.

I would therefore suggest that unless you have strong reasons for making the election it may be easier to come to an amicable agreement about who pays the tax bill.

Procedure

In cases where normal separate assessment would appear to be absolutely necessary you will want to know how to go about it. Application must be made by either husband or wife before the 6th July within the tax year for which it is to operate. It will continue in force for subsequent years until notice in writing is given to revoke it. This notice must be given before the 6th July, within the tax year for which it is no longer to have effect.

Separate taxation—wife's earnings

I mentioned earlier that a kind of partial separate assessment has been allowed since 1972/73, where the husband and wife jointly elect for it. When such an election is in operation, the wife's earned income is assessed on her as though she were a single person. The husband is assessed on his own income and any unearned income of his wife. They are both allowed the single personal allowance.

Before I go into further detail, I think it should be explained why it may be worth electing that the earned incomes shall be separated for tax purposes in this way. The answer is that so many wives are working these days and earning good money.

The normal situation in which the earnings of both husband and wife are aggregated may now lead to substantial higher rate tax. The separate treatment of the two amounts of earned income may leave them in a lower 'band' of income, and so attract a smaller percentage of tax.

The tax situation where an election has been made is this. The husband will be assessed on the whole of his income plus any unearned income of his wife. Against all this he is given only the single personal allowance, and forfeits the wife's earned income allowance. The wife is separately assessed as a single woman on her earnings only. She is given the single personal allowance.

Obviously, it is necessary to weigh up the pros and cons. For a start the total of two single allowances is not as much as the married personal allowance plus wife's earned income allowance. For 1978/79 this is £1970 against £2520, which means a loss in terms of tax relief of £181·50 (£550 @ 33%).

That is one thing. The better news in favour of this separate assessment on earnings is, as I have indicated, the opportunity to diminish the higher rate tax which would otherwise be payable. It must be obvious, therefore, that the husband's assessment on the joint incomes will attract higher rate tax, otherwise they must be out of pocket by reference to the tax relief of £181·50 which would be lost. It is necessary, therefore, to establish the kind of situation where the saving in higher rate tax exceeds this loss of tax relief.

Generally speaking, the 1978/79 joint income threshold, at which a separate election starts to become beneficial is about £12,450. For the married couple with two children under 11 and a £10,000 mortgage the figure is generally around £13,600. Due to the changes in the 1978 Finance Act the joint income level at which the election is worthwhile is probably higher than a year ago and it would be worthwhile to check the position again if you have already made an election.

However, the one thing to bear in mind is that there are no fixed limits to decide if an election is beneficial and the advice I would give is, if you think you may benefit, sit down and do a few sums on the following lines:

Example A—without the election

Husband's salary	£10,500
Wife's salary	£ 4500
	£15,000

Personal allowance	£1535		
Wife's earned income allowance	£ 985		
		£ 2520	
		£12,480	

£1500 @ 25%	£ 375·00
£6500 @ 33%	£ 2145·00
£1000 @ 40%	£ 400·00
£1000 @ 45%	£ 450·00
£1000 @ 50%	£ 500·00
£1480 @ 55%	£ 814·00
Total tax liability:	£ 4684·00

Example B—same circumstances but election in force

Husband	£10,500	
Less personal allowance	£ 985	
	£ 9515	
£ 750 @ 25%	£ 187·50	
£7250 @ 33%	£ 2392·50	
£1000 @ 40%	£ 400·00	
£ 515 @ 45%	£ 231·75	
		£3211·75
Wife	£ 4500	
Less personal allowance	£ 985	
	£ 3515	
£ 750 @ 25%	£ 187·50	
£2765 @ 33%	£ 912·45	
		£1099·95
Total tax liability:		£4311·70

The tax saved by this election is £372·30 and is made up as follows:

Savings in higher rate tax

£1480 @ 22%	£325·60
£1000 @ 17%	£170·00
£ 485 @ 12%	£ 58·20
	£553·80

Less loss on personal
allowances

£ 550 @ 33%	£181·50
Net Saving	£372·30

The election is obviously a good idea in this situation but lets have a look again at a couple who have the same joint income but the husband earns £13,000 and the wife £2000. The computation where no election has been made will obviously lead to the same tax liability as in Example A, i.e. £4684·00 but if an election is made the computation will read as follows:

Example C

Husband	£13,000	
Less personal allowance	£ 985	
	£12,015	
£ 750 @ 25%	£ 187·50	
£7250 @ 33%	£ 2392·50	
£1000 @ 40%	£ 400·00	
£1000 @ 45%	£ 450·00	
£1000 @ 50%	£ 500·00	
£1015 @ 55%	£ 558·25	
		£4488·25
Wife	£ 2000	
Less personal allowance	£ 985	
	£ 1015	
£ 750 @ 25%	£ 187·50	
£ 265 @ 33%	£ 87·45	
		£ 274·95
		£4763·20

The taxpayer here would be £79·20 worse off by making an election for separate taxation on earnings—and would obviously not do so. I think this makes the point that although the joint income is one factor which can help you decide that an election is beneficial you also have to take into account the distribution of the income between husband and wife.

In the previous examples I have been dealing with the situation where the wife's income is purely from earnings. However, the wife may have some investment income from capital and as I mentioned earlier even though an election has been made the investment income is still regarded as belonging to the husband. If we were to assume that the wife's income of £4500 in example B consisted of £4000 salary and £500 investment income, the tax payable if an election has been made is increased because £500 is added to his income and excluded for hers. The tax payable without the election would be the same.

A few other points to bear in mind if you make the election are that:

1. Life assurance relief is given to the spouse who pays the premiums.

2. If an allowance is claimed for a dependent relative the wife will get the allowance if she maintains her relative and this could be as much as the higher allowance of £145—men only get £100 (maximum).

3. Mortgage relief on a joint mortgage is normally allowed to the husband and this is generally the most beneficial arrangement as he usually has the higher taxable income. However, if the income position is reversed then it may be more beneficial if the wife has the mortgage relief. It would then be necessary to inform the Inspector of your decision.

I hope the above gives some idea what is involved in making the election for separate assessment of wife's earnings and demonstrates the financial benefits which can be obtained.

Procedure
The married couple living together must jointly elect if they so desire. The election may not be given earlier than 6 months before the beginning, or 12 months after the end of the year concerned.

It will continue in force until revoked, and notice of revocation may be given within 12 months of the end of the tax year for which it is to operate. The Inland Revenue may extend this 12-month period if circumstances warrant it. Form 14, obtainable from any tax office, is the one on which to elect, and form 14-1 revokes the election.

A final word on these elections:

Normal separate assessment does not save you money, it merely provides a certain amount of privacy for husband and wife and splits the tax bill in a 'fairer' way.

Separate assessment of wife's earnings, if correctly claimed, does save you money but provides none of the benefits of the other election.

Both elections can be claimed at the same time but I should warn you that the calculations arising from this computation are beyond the comprehension of all but the well informed few.

The last year of marriage

Within a tax year, a marriage may come to an end by the death of one of the spouses, by divorce, or by separation in circumstances which render permanent separation likely. There are certain points to be noted concerning the year in which a marriage ends.

1. For that year, the husband is entitled to the full married personal allowance. There is no reduction in this allowance if he marries again before the following 5th April.

2. The income of the wife is, for tax purposes, regarded as the husband's income up to the date of the ending of the marriage.

3. The wife is entitled to the whole of the single personal allowance against her income from the date of the ending of the marriage to the following 5th April.

4. Only one child allowance in respect of the same child can be claimed in the tax year during which the marriage ends. This may have to be apportioned as equitably agreed, or by reference to the contributions towards the upkeep of the child.

When tax collected from wife

One imagines that it is not generally known that, in certain circumstances, the Inland Revenue has the power to collect tax from a wife. Where income tax—or even capital gains tax—which has been assessed on the husband remains unpaid after 28 days from the due date, they may require payment of that tax by the wife.

Now I have no wish to scare wives into thinking that this is a regular procedure, or even that it will ever come to this. I should therefore explain further that this right of the Inland Revenue is bound up with what may be termed a notional appraisement of a formal separate assessment situation.

I realize that this may sound a little vague, but the position is this. Where the Commissioners of Inland Revenue consider that under a separate assessment election (even though no election has been made) an assessment could have been made on the wife, they may call upon her to pay the husband's outstanding tax, but only to the extent of the tax which could be ascribed to her under separate assessment.

Husband may disclaim liability

This is the husband's turn, but only, I regret, in sad circumstances. When a wife dies during the tax year, there may remain unpaid tax relating to her income whilst they were living together. The husband has no need to pay this unless, in the circumstances, he feels that he has a moral duty to do so. On the other hand, he has a perfectly legal right to give notice to his late wife's executors and his Inspector of Taxes, within two months after the grant of probate, that he wishes the Inland Revenue to collect from his late wife's estate tax calculated as if an election for separate assessment had been made.

Alimony and separation allowances

Small maintenance payments
Where Court Order payments for the maintenance of a divorced wife are regarded as 'small', the ex-husband making the payments is not required to deduct tax. The ex-wife is assessed to tax on such payments, if she is liable to tax at all. 'Small' is currently not exceeding £21 a week or £91 a month.

Where a Court Order maintenance payment is larger than the weekly or monthly sum mentioned above, tax at the basic rate is normally deductible from it. It is a charge on the income of the one paying it but, as the tax so deducted will have been retained, the gross amount of the payer's income will be assessed.

The one making the maintenance payment will have effectively saved himself basic rate tax on it. If there is higher rate tax to be paid on his income, the maintenance payment will also save him this—and at the highest rate at which he pays. For example:

Taxable income	£10,000	PAYE taxes	£3430
Less alimony	£ 1000	Tax retained	£ 330
Net taxable income	£ 9000	Tax suffered	£3100

It will be seen that the net taxable income has suffered tax at the basic 33%. As far as higher rate tax is concerned, there is only 7% to pay on £1000, i.e. £70. It is possible that PAYE might have accounted for this as well. It follows that the alimony payment has been instrumental in saving £450, that is £330 retained at source plus £120 (£1000 at 12%) reduction in PAYE tax, because this £1000, had it not been paid away in alimony, would have come into the second 'band' of higher rate tax. That is to say, the 45% band.

Capital gains tax
Although there is a section devoted to the preparation of statements for capital gains tax purposes in general, it would seem appropriate to deal with a small section of it here in order to complete the various tax situations of husband and wife.

For a married couple who are living together, calculations of capital gains and losses are made separately for each spouse, but any assessment on the net gains of the two together is made on the husband. The exception is for the year of marriage, in which the wife is assessed as a single person on any net gains which she herself may make.

There are, however, two instances of election for separate treatment. If application has been made for separate assessment, this will apply to the net gains or losses of each spouse separately. The other election is for any excess losses of the one *not* to be set against gains of the other. They may be carried forward to subsequent years. In both cases the election has to be made by the 6th July following the year for which it is to operate.

Disposals of chargeable assets between husband and wife who are living together do not create a situation where any action is necessary. They are merely 'internal' transfers, as it were, and the one who receives the asset is regarded as having acquired it at the amount which it cost the other. This applies to the year of marriage as well as any other year.

Where formal separate assessment in respect of Capital Gains Tax is in operation the total tax payable remains unchanged. The following examples demonstrate the principle for 1977/78 onwards:

Example A—without election

Husband	Gain	£1500
Wife	Gain	£2500
		£4000
Less exempt		£1000
Chargeable		£3000 @ 15% = £450

Without an election the bill for £450 will be sent to the husband.

Example B—election for separate assessment

Husband   Gain   £1500

Less exempt $\frac{1500}{4000} \times £1000$ £ 375

Chargeable   £1125 @ 15% = £168·75

Wife   Gain   £2500

Less exempt $\frac{2500}{4000} \times £1000$ £ 625

                                        ————
                                        £1875 @ 15% = £281·25
                                        ————————
                        Total liability   £450·00
                                        ————————

Once the election is in force the husband and wife will each receive a separate bill for the amounts indicated above.

Wife in employment

Maybe this heading should have been featured earlier on—if not first. The number of wives in employment does not appear to figure in my books of reference, but the £985 wife's earned income allowance is there for the taking—and, it would seem that it *is* taken by a goodly percentage of those who can escape from household chores and kids over play-school age.

Although, as I have so often said, the husband is legally the taxpayer for both himself and his wife who is living with him, the wife does find that, for the sake of expediency, tax is deducted by PAYE from her wages from employment.

This procedure has always slotted in well with the PAYE system. It suits the Inland Revenue in that it collects the tax readily and simply, and I feel sure that it meets with the approval of husbands. The wives appear to have come to terms with it.

The simplest 1978/79 notice of coding for a wife in employment will show total allowances due of £985, and code number 98. In some cases there may be an adjustment or two leading to a lower code number, but 98 will be the most usual.

For your guidance, code number 98 for 1978/79 would mean weekly tax deductions of about £3 from earnings of £30 a week, £4·50 from £35, and £6·00 from £40. This means that the average rate of tax is the very reasonable one of 10%, 13% and 15% respectively.

As I have said, it is convenient to let the wife's earned income allowance be allocated to a coding allotted to her separately. It should not be overlooked, however, that this allowance is legally an additional one granted to the husband in respect of his wife's earned income. This is an important principle to be borne in mind in cases where the husband's income does not absorb his full married personal allowance.

It may be unusual for a wife's income to be substantially greater than that of her husband but I think the situation should be exemplified. Let us assume that a husband in his forties becomes incapacitated and can no longer work. He has a few investments which bring in a gross £300 a year. His wife was a career woman and is now obliged to go back to her high-powered job which earns her £7000 a year.

The tax situation for 1978/79 would be as follows:

Husband	investment income		£ 300	Tax deducted £99
Wife	earned		£7000	
	Total income:		£7300	

Allowances
Married personal allowance— the husband being the legal taxpayer for both	£1535		
Wife's earned income allowance (maximum)	£ 985		
		£2520	
Taxable income		£4780	

£1500 @ 25%	£ 375·00
£3280 @ 33%	£1082·40
	£1457·40
Less tax deducted	£ 99·00
Tax liability:	£1358·40

In this situation the perfect coding would lead to deductions under PAYE of about £113 a month from the wife's earnings. Codings, however, are not always perfect—through no fault of the Inland Revenue or the taxpayer. They may have to be estimated by reference to what turns out to be inadequate information at the time they are due to be sent out.

It is worth mentioning, for the benefit of older taxpayers, that where a wife has contributed towards her own state pension, the wife's earned income allowance is due. For the benefit of the very young couple, however, I would add that this allowance is not due for the tax year in which the marriage takes place, unless the wedding happens to be on the 6th April—when it *is* due for the year ahead, and subsequently as long as the wife is earning.

Wife working for husband

Where a man is self-employed and works from his home address as his base, it is often the case that his wife is employed by him to carry out duties which are part of the running of the trade or profession. He will normally be paying her a fixed weekly or monthly salary, and the amount which she has been paid for the whole tax year will appear in his trading account as an expense.

During his examination of the trading account, the Inspector of Taxes will see that a salary has been paid to the wife and, by reference to the wife's duties as indicated in the account, will be satisfied as long as the salary is commensurate with those duties, and that the money is actually paid over.

There is one thing which must not be overlooked—but sometimes is. Where one of the expenses in the trading or professional account is 'wages paid to wife', the amount must appear in the husband's return in the section for income from employment. Where the husband is subject to higher rate tax, if the wages are more than the £985 maximum wife's earned income allowance, the excess will be part of the higher rate computation. If the wife has other employment, this may often be the case.

7

BUILDING SOCIETIES

Every financial institution has to balance its books—or, at any rate, endeavour to do so. Building Societies are no exception. Obviously they cannot lend money for house purchase and live on the interest alone. Their capital outlay is on the grand scale, and there has to be inflow of capital to match it.

The situation is met by the fact that the Building Societies are geared to act as banks as far as deposits of capital are concerned. That is to say, they run share accounts of various categories, from which depositors receive interest.

We have, therefore, the situation in which every Building Society both pays out and receives interest. This is the side of the business which impinges upon the tax situation of the individual. It is necessary, therefore, to discuss the impact upon both borrower and depositor.

Interest paid to Building Societies

Interest on a loan on mortgage for house purchase or improvement through a Building Society is always paid gross. The borrower cannot therefore obtain his tax relief by deducting tax and retaining the tax he deducts. This means that he must be given the appropriate tax relief by a deduction of the gross interest from his income before being charged to tax.

Loans from a Building Society are usually obtained on the basis whereby the borrower repays instalments of capital and pays the appropriate interest as the outstanding capital is reduced. The borrower knows this as a monthly sum which includes both capital repayments and interest.

Fortunately, for the purpose of completing the annual income tax return the borrower has no need to separate the two. The Building Society advises his tax office of the interest and the return merely calls for the name of the Society and the account or roll number.

Having been advised of the amount of the interest paid by the borrower in, say, 1978/79, the tax office has a note of it so that they are ready for the preparation of the appropriate assessment. The interest may be due to appear in a P70C assessment on earnings, or a Schedule D assessment. In either case, it appears as a deduction from income before tax is charged. It can be checked from the borrower's annual statement from the Building Society.

The payment of interest to a Building Society means that a legal charge for tax purposes on the borrower's income has been created. Where the total income is substantial, the saving in tax may well be at more than the basic 33%. For example:

Earnings, less allowances	£9000
Investment income	£ 800
	£9800
Less Building Society interest	£ 600
Taxable income	£9200

In this situation, the payment of £600 has saved not only basic rate tax at 33%, but higher rate tax as well. Thus:

Tax on the full £9800 is:	
£8000 @ basic & reduced rates	£2580
£1000 @ 40%	£ 400
£ 800 @ 45%	£ 360
	£3340
Less £600 @ 45%	£ 270
Tax liability	£3070

From this example, one can see that the borrower has saved £270. This is 45% of the interest. If he were paying interest at 8·5% to the Building Society, his effective rate, if my arithmetic has not let me down, is cut to 4·6%.

It will be appreciated, therefore, that the tax saving should be a major consideration in deciding what one can or cannot afford when contemplating a mortgage through a Building Society. Admittedly, my example was purposely set to take in some higher rate tax. Nonetheless, the 33% saving on a more down-to-earth income should similarly be considered. £198 would have been saved by the above borrower were he paying no more than basic rate tax. His effective interest rate would have been cut to 5·7%.

Interest received from Building Societies

There are two basic rules concerning interest received from a Building Society.

1. Through a special arrangement between the Societies and the Inland Revenue, basic rate tax is paid by the Society. No tax refund by reference to the interest can be claimed.

2. For tax purposes, the measure of a person's income from a Building Society is not the actual interest received. It is the gross equivalent calculated on the assumption that such interest has suffered tax at the basic rate. Thus for 1978/79, interest of £67 actually received is regarded as £100.

Dealing with (1) above the most significant factor which emerges is that this is unlikely to give the best return on your money if your income is too low to attract any tax at all. A good example of this would be a widow of 70 who's income is the state pension and £134 from her investment in the Building Society. Her spendable income for 1978/79 would be calculated as follows:

Pension	£ 950
Building Society interest (received net £134)	£ 200
	£1150
Age allowance	£1300
Tax liability	NIL
Pension	£ 950
Actual Building Society interest received	£ 134
Spendable income	£1084

However, if our widow had received £134 net from an investment in Local Authority Bonds, her spendable income would now be as follows:

Pension	£ 950
Local Authority interest	£ 200 (tax deducted £66)
Total income	£1150
Age allowance	£1300
Tax liability	NIL

She has still received £1084 but she also receives a tax repayment of £66. Thus, she is better off by £1·26 a week.

Now I am not suggesting for one moment that, generally speaking, a Building Society is not a good repository for your capital. In my view, theirs is a very satisfactory medium to provide a respectable return on any capital the ordinary person may wish to invest. If, as you should, you settle for a member of the Building Societies Association, you have safety for your capital, and no daily anxious glances at the 'yo-yo-like' activities in the City pages of your favourite newspaper.

One must be fair, however, and say that there is no growth for your capital with a Building Society. Does this matter? It depends on your temperament. I know that many people say that it does matter but, in my experience, they are the morons with their heads glued daily to the City pages instead of getting on with the process of living.

Another thing. Building Society interest, it is said, is not static. True enough—in the long term. For me, however, it remains static for long enough to keep a grip on the cost of living, and thus to dip into capital only as and when it becomes absolutely necessary to do so. Those who inherit are, in this day and age, usually well provided for and, in any case, often come into the proceeds of the sale of a house. At today's prices—that they should be so lucky!

We have now to discuss basic rule (2) mentioned earlier. That is to say, for tax purposes, the actual interest received has to be grossed up by a fraction of $\frac{100}{67}$. Thus, for 1978/79 interest of £67 actually received is regarded as £100. The gross figure of £100 is therefore deemed to have suffered basic rate tax and as long as the individual's income attracts no more than the basic rate tax no further tax will be due on this source.

However, where the individual is liable to higher rates and or investment income surcharge he can expect a bill from the Revenue for the extra tax due.

Here is a computation which shows the principle in action:

1978/79 Married man—2 young children
Earnings	£9500
Investment income	£1700 (tax at source £561·00)
Building Society	
interest received	£ 670 (tax to gross up £330·00)

1. *Earnings—(Tax Collected under PAYE)*   £9500

Less personal allowance	£1535		
Child allowance	£ 200		
		£1735	
Taxable income		£7765	
	£ 750 @ 25%		£ 187·50
	£7015 @ 33%		£2314·95
			£2502·45

2. *Investment income—(Tax collected by the issue of a taxed income assessment)*

  a) *Investment income surcharge*

Investment income	£1700
Building Society interest	
received £670 × $\frac{100}{67}$	£1000
Total	£2700
Less exempt	£1700
	£1000
£550 @ 10%	£55·00
£450 @ 15%	£67·50
	£122·50

b) *Higher Rate Tax*

Total investment income (as above)		£2700
Basic rate band	£8000	
Less used to cover earnings	£7765	
		£ 235
Liable to higher rates		£2465
i.e. £1000 @ 40%		£ 400
£1000 @ 50%		£ 500
£ 465 @ 55%		£ 255·75
Total		£1155·75
Less tax already paid at basic rate—£2465 @ 33%		£ 813·45
		£ 342·30
Total higher/additional rate bill		£ 464·80

8

DEALING WITH ENQUIRIES FROM YOUR TAX OFFICE

For the ordinary taxpayer, I am bound, from long experience, to say that the word 'enquiry' has a sinister ring about it. This is why I am devoting a chapter to it. I want to try and dispel the apprehension which it appears to engender. The ordinary honest taxpayer who completes his annual return to the best of his or her knowledge and belief need have no qualms about what lies behind an enquiry. This is what I hope to prove in the course of this chapter.

Inland Revenue Form 33

We have here one of the most basic enquiry forms sent out by the Inland Revenue. Quite painless to the recipient and very necessary to the tax office which issues it.

What happens is this. A certain tax office discovers that your address is in the area in which they operate. Don't ask me how. That is their business—and it doesn't matter anyway. They go on to say that they cannot trace any income tax papers for you. Fair enough. You may have recently moved into their district or changed your employment. They cannot do anything about dealing with your tax without your file which may be lying in a pigeonhole many miles away.

Anyway, they go on to suggest that your place of work or business may now be in another area. Or, if you do work in their area, your papers may be filed by reference to the name of your employer. This, surely, is a harmless enough enquiry to you, and the answer very necessary to them. Particularly as the last line on the front page reads 'will you kindly reply to the enquiries on the other side of this form and return it to me, please'. Note the word 'please'. If, after that, you drop form 33 into the waste paper basket you are doing yourself a disservice, and them a discourtesy.

My advice, therefore, which almost amounts to a request, is to turn over to the back of the form and to reply to the questions to the best of your ability. The questions are quite simple, and the material in your own tax file should readily supply the answers. There is no need for me to list them, because they are there for all to see who receive form 33. I can only repeat that those who do receive this form should complete it without delay, and post it under the franked label or envelope which comes with it.

Inland Revenue Form 41G

This is the enquiry form which asks for information concerning a taxpayer who, they understand, has set up in business on his own account. The tax office goes on to say that if this is the first time you have been in business on your own account 'you may like to call here to discuss any income tax points on which you are in doubt. If so, I shall be pleased to arrange an appointment'.

Could anything be more friendly and less sinister, than that? I would say not, and it is a good example of the Inland Revenue's latter years' approach to the problems of the ordinary taxpayer. Another is the marked simplification in the wording of forms and guides which is so welcome.

On the back of form 41G are the questions. Admittedly, there are eleven against the six on form 33, but it must be realized that a business, and all it entails, is obviously the subject of a fair amount of information. Here again, I need not quote the questions because they are self-explanatory. I cannot envisage anyone not being able readily to answer them.

Inland Revenue Form 46B

I am by no means privy to the internal machinery and prodecure of the Inland Revenue. I would hazard a guess, therefore, that the above enquiry is issued to a taxpayer who is self-employed, and who is somewhat late in lodging his annual income tax return.

I base this supposition on the fact that the form asks for a certified copy of the accounts for the last accounting year, together with the taxpayer's computation of the profits as adjusted for taxation purposes. In other words, the trading account which would have accompanied the annual return, had the latter been lodged in time for the tax office to raise the appropriate assessment at the time such assessments are normally made.

Fair enough. The tax office has a job to do, and without the current year's material to work on they cannot raise a precise assessment. It follows that if the return has, in fact, been over-looked for some time, form 46B should be complied with. That is to say, the trading account should be lodged without delay, and the full return completed as soon as possible afterwards.

The form goes on to say 'If the accounts have not been pre-pared, please state by what date a copy is likely to be available'. This gives the tax office the opportunity of gauging whether or not to consider the issue of an estimated assessment. No taxpayer wants this, with the subsequent bother of an appeal. I would suggest that an immediate reply to form 46B *may* obviate this estimate.

On the other hand, I have experienced estimated assessments where the return has been in the hands of the Inland Revenue for two months or more. This is a bit naughty. Obviously, it is something to do with the internal Revenue machinery, but it should not happen. If a return is with them within 30 days of its issue, there is no valid reason for an estimated assessment.

Before I leave the question of printed enquiry forms and, indeed, leave the Inland Revenue to rest in peace, I would mention that on more than one occasion I have been asked to complete form 33 where the taxpayer's affairs were already administered by the office which issued the form. This situation does, of course, make the hackles rise. The answer? Not to get too heated, but merely to write across the back of the form 'see Reference AB/1234'—or whatever.

A letter of enquiry

This, to most, is the sinister bit. But yet it need not cause pal-pitations of the heart. As I have often said, the tax office has a job to do. If, for example, they had been advised by your bank that you were credited with £85 by way of deposit interest in 1978/79, and no item appeared in your return under 'untaxed interest' for that year, what option have they but to ask you 'to consider whether income from all sources has been included'?

If it should be your lot to receive such a letter, don't panic. Just 'get considering'. Could there be any income which my conscientious return omitted? Oh, yes, of course. My bank manager suggested that I place on deposit the proceeds of the sale of my house pending the purchase of a smaller property.

There you are. Easily overlooked where no deposit account existed previously, but just as easily rectified. Write a note of sincere apology to your Inspector of Taxes, quoting the amount of the interest obtained from your bank. They may ask you for a certificate in writing that income from all sources has now been disclosed—but that will be that.

9

CONDUCTING A PERSONAL VISIT TO THE TAX OFFICE

A *personal* visit? I can imagine the raising of eyebrows and the rising of hackles at the very thought. Some appear not to want to know. Others can afford neither the fare, the petrol nor the time to visit Cardiff, Salford, Edinburgh, or wherever the overlords of decentralization have planted them.

You have, however, a *local* tax office. Everyone has—but 'local' can mean anything from almost on your doorstep to several miles away. You cannot expect the Board of Inland Revenue to settle for even a peppercorn rent to administer taxation to 50 inhabitants from a room in the local hostelry at Chipping Blankbury. The resultant increase in public expenditure would cause an outcry which would soon put paid to that kind of nonsense.

We are thus left with the most reasonable and sensible plan for tax administration that man has yet seen fit to devise. The policy has naturally to be tempered to fit in with the environment. That is to say, a commercially viable area may need to attract more tax offices which are equipped, staff-wise, to deal with company taxation.

It follows that you will never find tax offices in villages. Small towns usually have one. Larger towns, one or more, cities, several. Apart from which there are the decentralized offices at Cardiff, Edinburgh, Salford and so on. The forerunners of these remotely-located offices came into being during the war. It was a sensible evacuation programme which has expanded into a situation where local labour is more easily recruited than staff in London and the larger towns and cities.

What, then, is the answer to this situation where the tax office is so far away from the taxpayer who wants to know something? The situation has, in fact, been met as far as possible by the

Inland Revenue itself. There is a leaflet (form P509) which was first issued in 1972, and which has since been updated.

This leaflet came into being specifically to meet the requirements of those in employment whose tax offices had departed seemingly to the ends of the earth. In short, it recognizes that this centralization of PAYE work has made it impossible for an employee to 'pop in' and sort out, verbally, a difficulty over coding, change of job, or whatever. It sets out, in fact, a list of local enquiry offices offering general advice and assistance on PAYE matters.

These enquiry offices are geared to answer anything concerning the machinery of PAYE in a general way. You may, of course, turn round and say that you don't want an answer 'in a general way'. Yours is a specific question which applies to you personally. Your wife didn't give birth on the 5th April 'in a general way'. She did it for *me*, and I would like to know about my tax refund. How much will it be, and when may I expect it?

Fair enough on the surface, I suppose. We all seem to imagine that *our* tax affairs are something special at the tax office. A cut above those earmarked for general treatment, no less. This is a natural assumption, but if you think about it a bit, and even hear me out, you will come to realize that probably 99% of PAYE enquiries can be satisfactorily resolved by reference to the general principles applicable to the system.

Having said that, you will appreciate that in the other 1% of cases there may be special circumstances whereby the local enquiry office would feel it necessary to have a sight of your own particular file. Should this be necessary, they will send for it, and will get in touch with you again to tell you that the file has surfaced. You have then only to call again, and all will be revealed.

So far, we have been referring only to PAYE situations. There are, of course, others. Many taxpayers have untaxed interest which is assessed under Schedule D. Fortunately, this situation is often resolved by the fact that both Schedule D and Schedule E are administered by the same tax district. There may be two distinct files, but they will be linked by cross-reference.

This appears to be the case where there is a pension from the public sector, a state pension and untaxed income. The chances are that the taxpayer's files will be tucked away at Cardiff. That admirable city does happen to be somewhat beyond the range from which a personal visit would be possible—unless, of course, you just happen to live in Llanishen.

Seriously though, your local enquiry office can satisfy most customers. Admittedly, without your file, they cannot tell you off the cuff why your P70C shows that your tax was underpaid by, say, £57·50 at the 5th April 1979. This is an explanation which must come by letter from the tax office which holds your file. They can tell you how and why your code number failed to collect the requisite tax for 1978/79; hopefully, it will be 'coded in' for 1979/80, and you will not have to find the tax due by way of a lump sum.

Some of us—myself included—are fortunate enough to be assessed under Schedule D by a reasonably local tax office. This is a base where personal visits may not be too much of a problem. Although my Schedule E assessments emanate from far-away Salford, I find that my local tax office is most helpful. They are constantly in touch with Salford, and can answer anything within a few days—if not immediately. Even so, my 'local' office is 16 miles away, but that will do for as long as I can handle a car safely—and afford to run it.

I recognize only too well that the elderly, the infirm, and the disabled, have a problem over any visit at all to a tax office. It may well be quite out of the question. I have already mentioned this in the chapters dealing with the completion of returns and claims. I am, however, discussing a personal visit to one's tax office, and I must therefore assume that you are able to make your way there—either alone, or by the courtesy and kindness of a friend or relative.

It will make life a lot easier for you if you know what to take with you to a tax office. If you have a tax file (and I always imagine that everyone has), it obviously has top priority. Take the *whole* file—not merely a few bits and pieces out of it. Furthermore, have a look around the home to make sure that there is nothing 'awaiting filing'. If there is, take that as well.

If you don't have a tax file, as such, you should certainly take with you whatever it is you are going to see them about. It may be a letter which you have received and don't understand, a notice of coding or assessment which you are questioning. Whatever it is, take it with you.

The reason I am stressing the fact that you should have with you anything which you have received and don't understand is that the tax office's reference will be on it. On a personal visit to your tax office your reference number must go with you. It is not a bad idea to keep a note of it in your wallet or handbag. If you happen to 'pop in' while passing, your reference number will be your passport to a speedy reply. You may get away with it by naming your employers, but don't bank on it.

I think it might be helpful to many of you if I get down to a few imaginary conversations between a member of the Inland Revenue staff (IR) and a member of the public (MP).

An addition to the family

MP   Good morning.

IR   Good morning.

MP   I thought I should let you know that we had another son last Thursday, June 24th.

IR   Congratulations! May I have your tax reference.

MP   Certainly. I have it here.

IR   Good. I expect you know that this means that you are entitled to a further child allowance for 1978/79 of £100.

MP   I rather thought this would be the case, but do I get it straight away?

IR   There is no reason why its effect should not be felt without delay. We will give you a new code number, and for every month up to 5.4.79 your PAYE deduction will be less than it is now. In fact, your tax deduction at the 31st July should be £11 less, and your pay chits for the following months should show an increase of about £2·75.

MP   Thank you. Is there anything which I have to do?

IR   If you will just complete and sign this child allowance claim, we will advise your employers of your revised code number.

MP   There. You make even a birth quite painless.

IR   Just a part of the service, I assure you.

Change of employment

MP   Good morning.

IR   Good morning.

MP   I am shortly changing my job. I am employed at the moment by Berrylows, the undertakers. Your reference is B999. At the end of this month, I start work with Living, Still & Company of Oxbridge. What do I have to do about my tax?

IR   When you leave Berrylows ask them for form P45. This form should be produced to your new employers when you start work with them. This will ensure continuity of your PAYE tax deductions at the appropriate rate.

MP   Do you deal with employees of Living, Still & Co?

IR   No, but your file will, in due course, be transferred to Oxbridge 2nd district and they will deal with your tax affairs as long as you remain in that employment.

MP   So there is nothing further for me to do other than hand over P45 to my new employers?

IR   Not at the moment. You will receive your next annual return for completion from Oxbridge 2.

MP   Thank you.

I should perhaps mention, at this point, that if, in the above example, the employee, after leaving, has no further employment in mind at the moment, his present employer should also give him a form P50 on which to claim any refund of tax arising as a result of his unemployment.

Estimated assessment

MP   Good afternoon.

IR   Good afternoon, madam.

MP   I received this estimated assessment on £200 for untaxed interest a few days ago. Can you tell me, please, why this should have been sent to me because I happen to know that my interest from the Special Investment account and 3% Savings Bonds in 1978/79 will be nowhere near this £200?

IR   Just a moment, and I will have a look at your file—(*pause for 3 or 4 minutes.*)
   Oh! yes, I can see why we had to send this out. I'm afraid that we do not appear to have received your 1978/79 return.

MP   Oh! dear. I do remember receiving some form or other from you some time ago, but I'm afraid I must have put it on one side and I have obviously forgotten all about it. In any case, how does it tie up with this estimated assessment?

IR   Well, the 1978/79 return calls for the income of 1977/78, and it is the income of 1977/78 which has legally to form the basis for the assessment for 1978/79. In the absence of a return of income for the year on which we base the assessment, we have to make an estimate to the best of our ability. Your untaxed income in 1976/77 was £175, and, in our experience, such income does appear to increase year by year. It was thus estimated that £200 would be reasonable.

MP   Yes, I understand. I do apologize for not having completed the return, but what do I do now?

IR   The first thing for you to do is to lodge an appeal. Hold on a moment and I will give you the necessary form. Here we are. This is form 64-7S—although you probably received one with the estimated assessment. I will give you a hand with completing it. There. If you will just sign it here.

MP   Thank you. Anything else?

IR   Well, if we may now have your current return as soon as possible. When we get it, we shall cancel the estimated £200 assessment and replace it by a revised one in accordance with the untaxed interest in the return about to be completed.

MP   I shall let you have the return within a day or two.

IR   Good. Thank you.

The wrong approach

(1) By the taxpayer

MP   I've got a letter from you here. I like neither its tone nor its implication. Get me someone in authority who knows what he's doing, will you.

IR   Certainly. If you will just wait a moment I will find the officer dealing with your case.

MP   Officer? What do you mean—officer? This isn't the Army, you know. More's the pity. Might get something done efficiently if it were—for a change.

IR   It happens to be a term used within the Inland Revenue and applies to certain grades among the staff. Anyway, I will get him for you.

Interval of precisely 1½ minutes

IR   Good morning. Can I help you?

MP   I doubt it—but it's worth a try. I have received this letter which asks me to consider carefully whether all sources of income have been disclosed in the return which I sent you some weeks ago. I don't know what you are getting at, but I am not in the habit of evading tax.

IR   We are not suggesting this for a moment, but we do have information in our possession which leads us to believe that your return may not be quite complete.

MP   Do you indeed? The snoopers have been at it again, I suppose. And what, pray, is this precious information which leads you to this sinister conclusion?

IR   It is not the policy of the department . . .

MP   I bet it isn't!

IR   If I may be allowed to continue, I was saying, in effect, that there is no need at this stage to indicate exactly what we believe has been omitted from a return. We are merely asking you—politely, I thought—if, on reconsideration, you can recall any item of income which may inadvertently have been overlooked.

MP   What sort of income?

IR   Well, have you considered, for instance, your account with your stockbrokers?

MP   My stockbrokers? Of course I have. My capital transactions and acquisitions were set out accurately in the statement which went with the return.

IR   I quite agree, but I gather that your account with them was at one time substantially in credit pending a favourable opportunity for investment.

MP   So what? Many investors must be in the same situation, but what has this got to do with my return?

IR   Well, some stockbrokers allow interest on accounts which are, from time to time, substantially in credit. Yours appears to be one of them.

MP   Does it now? And how would you know about that?

IR   In certain circumstances, there is a legal obligation on the part of institutions to report any interest which has been paid without deduction of tax.

MP   I don't remember any interest. If there was any, I suppose it must be hidden away somewhere among the computerized statements which I get from my stockbrokers from time to time. How much is it supposed to be then— if you know so much about it?

IR   That is not for the department to say. We look to you, as

	the taxpayer, to render a return which includes any untaxed interest which has been received during the year.
MP	I see. So you're not telling. Typical. I suppose I now go home and delve among my computerized statements to find some piffling amount of interest, the amount of which you already know.
IR	If you would, please. Perhaps you would kindly advise us by letter of the amount of the interest, and confirm at the same time that, to the best of your knowledge and belief, income from every source has now been disclosed.
MP	I was waiting for that bit. We are back with the tone of your original letter. Obviously you have a job to do, but I didn't like the letter. Anyway, you will be hearing from me.
IR	Thank you.

Comment

This is a disgraceful example of indefensible aggressive repartee by a member of the public who has received a polite and completely justifiable letter from his tax office. Mind you, I have heard this kind of thing many times. Not these precise words, obviously, but a tirade equally inexcusable.

All right, you may say, but what would have been an appropriate approach in these circumstances? My view, for what it is worth, is this. The Inland Revenue does not write letters for fun. They are public servants who are at all times governed in their actions by the rule of tax law.

If I had received such a letter, I should not, for a start, have visited, or written to, my tax office until I had taken a long cool look at my copy of the last return, and the material from which I had constructed it. You may argue that I am used to this sort of thing. Of course I am. It is my job to be. Nonetheless, there is no reason why I should not pass on the benefit of experience, and this is, naturally, my aim and object with this book.

From the general tone of such a letter, I would immediately have suspected an omission of untaxed interest. If, after racking such brains with which I have been endowed, and a thorough examination of relevant material in my file, I was still unable to trace any omission in my return, I would say so, either verbally or by letter, and ask the tax office if they could see their way to be a little more explicit.

The result would, of course, have been the same. They would have stretched a point by a veiled reference to my stockbrokers' account, and an apology would have settled the matter on an amicable basis.

(2) By the Inland Revenue

MP   (*a widow*) I have a claim form here. I am afraid that I have made rather a mess of it. Do you think that I may have another form? I do like to send in a claim which is reasonably clear, and I am not sure that you would understand it as it is.

IR   Just a minute. I will enquire.

5 minute interval—another IR official comes up to the counter

IR   What exactly is it you want?

MP   I have already explained to your colleague that I would like another claim form R40.

IR   Another one? We sent you a claim form with your last repayment order.

MP   I know you did, but, as I have also explained, I have made rather a mess of it, and I think it would be better for us both if I complete a new form.

IR   This is not usual, you know. We don't issue claim forms to just anyone. It is not our policy. We have already issued form R40 in accordance with our instructions and we don't normally issue another to the same individual. What's the matter with the original form, anyway? Have you got it here?

MP   Yes, here it is.

IR   Well, I don't see anything wrong with that. There are a few crossings-out, admittedly, but I can't really see that we could not understand it. We are used to this sort of thing, you know.

MP   Yes, you may be, but I happen to be rather particular about the completion of forms for any purpose, and I am certainly not satisfied with this. After all, I have to sign it, and I will only sign something with which I am satisfied.

IR   Suit yourself, but give me back the form which you have already completed, and I will obtain another for you.

MP   Thank you. I will let you have this new form back as soon as possible.

IR   There is no hurry. A claim such as this is your business.
        You have the right to make it if you want to.

Comment

It will be understood that the conversation as above must be
digested for what it is. That is to say, a figment of my imagination.
It is, however, broadly based upon long experience of dealing
personally with the Inland Revenue. Let it be said loudly and
clearly, however, that for, say, 95% of the time, I have received
nothing but courteous assistance from tax offices everywhere.

With that firmly established, I feel justified in saying that on a
few very isolated occasions over 30 odd years of experience, I
have run up against situations which I have endeavoured to
crystallize into an imaginary interview.

A claim on form R40 is a legal right given to the taxpayer. It
exists in order that overpaid tax may be wrested from the Inland
Revenue, to whom it cannot be said to belong. The widow in my
example was not satisfied that her completion of the form would
be clear to the authorities. It is my understanding that tax offices
must be bedevilled by many thousands of claims and returns
which are ambiguous and may therefore lead to unnecessary
correspondence.

This widow was merely trying to be helpful. The fact that claim
forms are not dished out left, right and centre is irrelevant in the
circumstances. The Inland Revenue is serving the public, and the
public are entitled to courtesy where they are endeavouring to be
helpful.

10

YOUR QUESTIONS ANSWERED

It has often been brought home to me that you may be in for some awkward situations if you so much as drop a hint as to what you do. You don't shout it from the housetops, of course, but a snippet of careless talk at a party can bring in its wake situations which give one food for thought.

ACQUAINTANCE	You know about tax, I believe.
ME	Well, I am supposed to.
ACQ.	You wouldn't mind if I just asked you something, would you?
ME	Well, I don't usually answer anything off the cuff.
ACQ.	Naturally, I quite understand, but this would be simple to you. I haven't a clue about these things.
ME	Well, what's the trouble?
ACQ.	I have had a demand for tax of £x which I am sure cannot possibly be right. I thought that Building Societies were supposed to pay your tax for you?

At this stage, one has to think quickly. Has it to be 'You should really appoint a tax adviser, you know' and risk being marked down as a bad neighbour? Or should one settle for the good Samaritan bit and go further into the matter?

I may be in the minority, but I have always made it a point never to glean information through the back door. Others seem to be less inhibited. In a devious sort of way, I suppose I should be grateful, because a casual question over the garden wall, or wherever, has led to a kind of mental dossier embracing the more common questions asked by the ordinary individual. Hence this chapter—which I hope will be helpful.

Why is tax so complicated?
With, perhaps, one or two exceptions, tax is not particularly complicated for the ordinary person with earnings or a pension, a few investments and perhaps one or two odds and ends of other income. There must be rules, or the collection of tax would be a haphazard thing which would lead to widespread dissatisfaction among taxpayers everywhere.

You may argue that there is already dissatisfaction. It does exist—and we all know it. Fringe benefits, and that sort of thing. The executive and the director with his company car, and seemingly unlimited expenses allowed for this, that and the other.

Fair comment, but look how Chancellors in recent years have made it impossible for the loaded taxpayer to get away with this kind of thing without being liable to tax on the monetary value, or the money itself. In a nutshell, it is the loopholes which hawk-eyed taxpayers have unearthed over the years which our over-lords, in dogmatic fashion have plugged, in order that those whose employment attracts no such benefits will not be worse off than the 'privileged' who were, at one time, 'getting away with it'.

This is only one example, but there were—and are—others which, in the view of successive Chancellors, have needed what they termed careful study. Companies' activities, the making of settlements, VAT and CTT have come in lately for most of this attention, but these complicated provisions do not impinge to a very noticeable extent upon the ordinary individual.

Having said that, I hope I shall not be accused of condoning the mass of taxation legislation already in existence, and the grossly overweight Finance Acts which are thrown at us every year. Nothing could be further from my thoughts on the matter. We who deal with taxation were bitterly disillusioned when the 1970 Taxes Act failed to do anything but consolidate all that had gone before. A great opportunity was lost. We wanted a simple Act, with vision instead of a studied determination to bemuse, and to prevent even a hint of evasion in scores of situations where the tax saved would not be worth a light to the Treasury.

I could go on—but this is not a soapbox. You wanted to know why the taxation system seems to be so complicated to the man-in-the-street. The answer is that the Inland Revenue have such a monstrous pile of complicated legislation on their plate that a finely-disciplined form-ridden system is absolutely essential to the collection of each individual's legal share of the tax burden.

Why is the tax office so long in replying to letters?

I think this question has to be answered by reference to my knowledge of the tax system generally, and from my own experience of a situation which I happen to know does rankle with the taxpaying public.

In the first place, shortage of staff—and trained staff at that—obviously makes for delay in replying to letters. Why should there be any shortage, you may ask. I happen to know that the holidays are quite generous and the pensions up to the average. Arguably, a safe job. Why, therefore, are recruits backward in coming forward?

I think the answer lies in the fact that you have necessarily to be the type of person who is willing to serve the public. That this is a doubtful privilege must surely be borne out by some of the indefensibly aggressive behaviour by the public, not only in Inland Revenue offices, but in Post Offices, Social Security offices and so on.

It follows that letters from the public have to take their turn in the queue. The length of time taken to reply to letters from taxpayers depends upon a number of facts:

(a) The number of letters—obviously.
(b) The clarity of the letters.
(c) The complexity of the letters.
(d) The person-power situation in a particular section of the tax office in question.

As one who has dealings with a large number of tax offices, I have obviously a greater opportunity of weighing up the general situation than an individual whose only experience relates to one tax district. The extent of delay varies widely. One has one's pet tax districts where both the tone of letters and the immediacy with which correspondence is dealt engender a warm-hearted appreciation leading to a two-way rapport. This, of course, is taxation practice at its best.

The other side of the coin may, perhaps, not be in quite such mint condition, but one endeavours to make allowances for the reasons stated above. I know only too well that where there appears on the surface to be no reason for a long delay, one can become slightly hot under the collar. I think the answer here has to be a polite reminder that this delay in replying is causing one to lose the drift of the subject matter when the original object was to try and get something settled to mutual advantage.

Can I obtain help with the completion of my tax return or claim?

The short answer is, of course, yes. To expand this, however, it is necessary to know the circumstances of the one who is asking the question. It may be that he or she is elderly, mentally or physically incapacitated, or even blind. It may be someone who is merely wondering whether it is the practice of the tax office to give assistance at the counter. Or, in the last resort, there are those who want to leave it all to someone qualified to do it.

Those who are incapable of the completion of a return or claim do have a problem. This applies particularly to a claim because the refund expected is so often absolutely essential for the maintenance of the claimant. In my experience, relatives are very good in this situation, but they do, of course, have to know about the plight of the incapacitated person. It is very sad if a refund of tax should be left unclaimed merely because nobody—relative or friend—happens to know that a refund of tax is, in fact, due.

Fortunately, I would suggest that this very seldom happens where the incapacitated person is in a hospital or a nursing home. The almoner will be aware of a patient's financial circumstances, and will know of those cases where taxed income is being received. Relatives or friends who are willing to help are contacted, and they are usually able to come to the rescue.

A signature on a claim or return is occasionally not possible—and yet the Inland Revenue must have one. Whilst a very rough and scratchy signature, just recognizable to the tax authorities, is normally acceptable, a cross will just not do. The solution here is for a relative or friend to take out a Power of Attorney. The attorney's signature is then accepted, and any tax refund will be paid over to him or her for subsequent transfer to the incapacitated person.

For those who are able to pay a visit to the tax office there always appears to be willing assistance. It is, of course, incumbent upon the taxpayer to complete a return or claim as far as possible. In some cases, however, one or two of the sections may give rise to uncertainty. The notes for guidance with claims and returns usually state that assistance will be given where difficulty is experienced.

There is a kind of 'middle-of-the-road' course open to those who cannot afford to employ a professional agent, but who come up against the occasional problem in the process of doing their own tax work. They would be well advised to join the Income Tax Payers' Society.

This Society was founded in 1921 and, with a resident team of taxation experts, provides a very comprehensive advisory service to anyone with a tax problem. They are located at 1st Floor, 5 Plough Place, Fetter Lane, London EC4A 1XN—Telephone 01-583 8181.

The cost, in this day and age, is very reasonable—far below that which would have to be found if one appointed an accountant as tax agent. For example, a private subscriber pays £10 in the first year, and only £8 thereafter. There are varying rates for professional and overseas members. Full particulars of these and, in fact, of the Society's entire services and activities can be found in the latest leaflets obtainable from them.

Finally, there are some who have reached the stage where they don't want to be bothered any longer with their taxation commitments, and are willing and able to pay for someone to act for them. How do they set about this, and what does it involve—and cost?

The procedure here is to contact The Institute of Chartered Accountants in England and Wales, The Institute of Taxation or the Association of Certified Accountants. As you would expect, they are both based in London, and may, of course, be found in the telephone directory for the London postal area.

The former body has, however, eighteen District Societies, and it would be an obvious move to get in touch with the one nearest to you. This makes future contact with an accountant more simple. The Institute of Taxation is in London only, but they will put you in touch with a qualified taxation practitioner in your area who would be willing to act for you. Whichever you choose, you may rest assured that your tax affairs will be dealt with to your satisfaction.

The cost? This depends entirely upon the complexity of your tax affairs, the amount of correspondence, and the time spent over a tax year. It would be unethical for me to forecast a figure which could vary widely according to circumstances. You might, however, be able to obtain an estimate based broadly upon the facts which you are prepared to furnish when applying.

Do I do anything if I have not received a return form for completion?
Do we all receive a return form for completion? Normally, yes. For one reason or another, however, a return is occasionally not received, and I am often asked if one should do anything about this. The answer, by reference to tax law, is quite plain. If you have not lodged a return for any particular year, you are obliged to give notice to your tax office—within twelve months of the end of that tax year—that you are chargeable to tax.

Chargeable to tax? How do I know that I am, you may ask. A good question, but tax law does not answer it exactly for us. The assumption is that we are all able to decide whether or not we are chargeable to tax. If you know you are, your duty is clear. Contact your local tax office. In any case, liaison with your Inspector of Taxes will determine whether or not he requires any action from you. If you do this you are in the clear. Neither ignorance of the law nor the fact that you received no return form would excuse you from the penalties which can follow failure to give notice of liability to tax, or to complete the return which would normally follow.

I stress the importance of the annual return because its lodgment as soon as possible after the 5th April in each year is so necessary. Necessary not only to the Inland Revenue, but to you yourself, in order to be sure of every relief from tax to which you are legally entitled. The accurate completion of the return is the only way of ensuring this.

What is the difference between Allowances and Reliefs?

Allowances
I would define an allowance as a deduction from gross income to which every individual is legally entitled according to his or her circumstances. That is to say, a deduction represented by the total allowances due, so that the tax liability is calculated on the remainder of the gross income. This remainder is the taxable income.

From what I have said in earlier chapters you will know that allowances are labelled according to the circumstances for which they are granted. The single personal allowance is everyone's minimum—the other allowances being additional deductions which have to be claimed in the appropriate section(s) of the annual return.

Reliefs

The reactions of most of you are, I think, predictable. Surely, you must be thinking, *allowances* deducted from gross income lead effectively to *relief* from tax. In short, cause and effect.

A finely-drawn distinction, I admit, but I see it like this. Allowances reduce the income, on which tax is then calculated. Relief from tax is a further reduction in the tax liability which was calculated initially by reference to allowances alone.

The prime example is life assurance relief. At one time, the reduction, for premiums paid, of the tax otherwise due was given in the form of an allowance deductible along with the other allowances. It is now definitely a relief because, at the end of an assessment, the tax due is reduced a little further by the amount of the allowable premiums at half the basic rate.

Another example is relief for annual interest paid. Admittedly, those with a mortgage will be accustomed to finding a deduction in their assessments for Building Society interest paid. This is done, however, merely for convenience. It is still tax relief for interest paid, and it could just as well be converted into tax at one's highest rate and deducted from the tax otherwise found to be due.

APPENDIX

Budget Changes Effective from 1979/80

APPENDIX

Budget Changes Effective from 1979/80

The difficulties encountered by the individual in understanding his income tax situation are compounded by frequent changes not only in the rates of income tax and allowances but also in the ground rules affecting his taxability. Such changes usually result from shifts in Government fiscal policy. However, a further factor rendering change inevitable in recent years has been the high level of inflation which has led to a regular erosion of the value of allowances and tax rate bands stated in fixed amounts. This was the background to the so-called 'Rooker-Wise' amendment accepted by the Government during the discussion stages on the 1977 Finance Act, under which it became committed to regular increases in the rates of personal allowances to coincide with increases in the retail price index.

Recent years have seen a departure from the situation where a Budget statement could be expected from the Chancellor of the Exchequer early in April giving details of changes which could be regarded with some confidence as being those operative for the remainder of the fiscal year. In 1977 a proposed reduction in the basic rate of income tax to 33% announced on 29th March was made conditional upon reaching a satisfactory agreement on a new pay policy. The final outcome was that basic rate was only reduced to 34% but some personal allowances were increased a second time by further action in July so that changes in pay codes only became operative in August. In 1978 a reduction in the basic rate of income tax to 33% was finally accepted by the Government in July although no reduction had been proposed in the April Budget.

With the fall of the Labour Government and the announcement of a General Election for 3rd May, it became obvious that in 1979, once again, certainty over tax rates and allowances for the year would be delayed possibly for several months. As one of its last acts the outgoing Government introduced a brief Finance Act, which received the Royal Assent on 4th April, mainly as a holding measure to continue in force the tax rates effective for the previous year. It also introduced certain changes in personal allowances for 1979/80 to fulfil its commitment under the Rooker-Wise amendment.

Once the result of the General Election was known, it seemed certain that more substantial changes were on the way and it was decided that publication of this book should be deferred until after the Budget statement on 12th June in order to incorporate details of those changes. The new rates showing, for comparison, the 1978/79 rates and the rates originally proposed for 1979/80 are summarised below:—

Personal Allowance – 1979/80

	New 1979/80 Rates	1979/80 Rates Originally Proposed	1978/79
Personal Allowance			
Single	£1165	£1075	£985
Married	£1815	£1675	£1535
Wife's Earned Income Allowance	£1165	£1075	£985
Age Allowance			
Single	£1540	£1420	£1300
Married	£2455	£2265	£2075
(Income limit)	£5000	£4400	£4000
Additional Personal Allowance	£650	£600	£550

In most cases, the changes brought about by these increases will be given effect to, for those in employment, on the first pay day after 12th July bringing a welcome tax refund because the changes are effective from 6th April.

Basic Rate Income Tax

A further Budget change is the reduction in the Basic Rate of Income Tax from 33% to 30% with effect from 6th April. If you are in employment, the benefit of this reduction will not be felt until after 5th October because it takes some time to print new tax tables but there should then be a further tax refund for you. If you have received other income since 6th April from which tax has been deducted at 33% you will either receive credit for the overdeduction the next time you receive income from the same source or will need to claim repayment from the Inland Revenue.

Higher Rates of Income Tax

Along with the reduction of Basic Rate, there has been an easing of the Higher Rates of Income Tax payable on larger incomes involving not only a reduction of the highest rate from 83% to 60% but also an extension of the bands of income on which the differential rates are charged.

Income Tax Rates – 1979/80

Rate of tax %	1979/80 taxable income £	1978/79 taxable income £
25	0–750	0–750
30	751–10000	
33		751–8000
40	10001–12000	8001–9000
45	12001–15000	9001–10000
50	15001–20000	10001–11000
55	20001–25000	11001–12500
60	over 25000	12501–14000
65		14001–16000
70		16001–18500
75		18501–24000
83		over 24000

Investment Income Surcharge – 1979/80

Rate of surcharge %	1979/80 All individuals – investment income £	1978/79 Under 65– investment income £	1978/79 65 and over – investment income £
10		1700–2250	2500–3000
15	over 5000	over 2250	over 3000

The changes for 1979/80 mean that nobody, whether under or over 65, will pay Investment Income Surcharge on a joint investment income not exceeding £5000.

Other Income Tax Changes – 1979/80
If you have been claiming a deduction for interest paid on a loan taken out before 27th March 1974, where eligibility for relief was expected to cease at 5th April 1980, you are now given two more years in which to claim the relief for interest paid up to 5th April 1982.

Social Security Payments
The standard rate of retirement pension is to be increased from November 1979 by £6·10 to £37·30 for a married couple and by £3·80 to £23·30 for a single person. At the same time the premium for one parent families claiming child benefit will be increased from £2 to £2·50.

Tax Payable at different levels of Income – 1979/80

Income	Tax Payable			
	Single Persons		Married Couples	
	under 65	over 65	under 65	over 65
£	£	£	£	£
Income all earned				
4000	813	700	618	426
4500	963	850	768	576
5000	1113	1000	918	726
6000	1413	1413	1218	1218
7000	1713	1713	1518	1518
8000	2013	2013	1818	1818
9000	2313	2313	2118	2118
10000	2613	2613	2418	2418

Income half earned, half from investments

15000	4963	4963	4671	4671
20000	7780	7780	7455	7455
25000	10847	10847	10489	10489

This table gives a general guide to the amounts of tax payable by individuals in different circumstances and at different levels of income but it should be borne in mind that most people are able to make claims for other items such as mortgage interest relief or dependent relative relief which will further reduce their tax liability.

Conclusion

Although this Budget will make a marked difference to the burden of direct taxation suffered by most people it is relatively free of changes in principle with the result that by following the guidance I have attempted to give you in this book and applying the new rates of tax and allowances, you should be able to calculate your tax liabilities and to take advantage of legitimate opportunities for reducing them.

No changes have been made in the rates or rules relating to Capital Gains Tax but the Chancellor has referred to a review of the basis of taxation of capital and I fear that such changes can be expected in a forthcoming Budget.

EDUCATION A-Z

More *Daily Telegraph* books published by Collins

Education A–Z is a comprehensive guide to our education system that will help parents, teachers and senior pupils.

Education A–Z is a dictionary of over 400 topics from the world of education, types of school, teaching methods, key reports and papers, pressure groups, teachers' organizations. Special treatment is given to current problems such as violence, bullying, size of classes, politics in education, streaming, truancy, uniforms, etc. Subjects covered range from nursery schools and pre-school playgroups to universities and further education.

Education A–Z will help parents understand the vocabulary of modern schooling methods.

Education A–Z will help students decide between the bewildering range of educational opportunities after age 16.

Education A–Z will help practising teachers and those still training keep up to date with the latest reports and ideas.

Education A–Z will help everybody who is interested in education in Britain today.

John Izbicki has been Education Correspondent of *The Daily Telegraph* since 1969 and has assembled here the answers to hundreds of questions he is asked regularly by anxious parents.

Home Ownership
A-Z

Home Ownership A–Z is a clear, straightforward guide to buying, selling and owning a home of one's own. Part one takes the reader step by step through the process of choosing and buying a home, be it cottage, flat, modern semi, terrace house or detached residence. The actual operations involving solicitors, estate agents, and building societies are all clearly explained. Part two is a comprehensive encyclopedia of terms and procedures connected with the purchase and ownership of residential property from auctions to woodworm, bridging loans to rateable value, and from fences to freehold, with helpful explanations.

The result is a particularly valuable handbook for everybody considering home ownership and who would like to know precisely how to go about it and what it entails.

Arthur Bowers has been writing on property matters for over twenty years for *The Daily Telegraph* and has therefore been able to draw on unrivalled experience of the actual problems people face in obtaining and maintaining their own home.

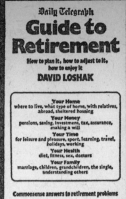

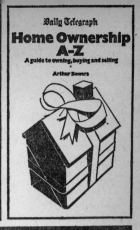

Guide to Retirement

Retired? — Are you enjoying life?
About to retire? — Are you looking forward to every minute of it?
Are your parents approaching retirement age?

Far too many dread retirement as the end of the road, a withdrawal from work and activity, from friends and companions. The whole idea is depressing and seems to be surrounded by a taboo that inhibits discussion.

This book makes a very positive approach to the subject of retirement, highlights the opportunities that freedom from work brings, and suggests many ways to take advantage of them.

The important questions of house and home, whether to stay put or move, whether to live abroad or with relatives are all evaluated. Money matters, taxation, annuities, assurance are all explored and the author gives advice on how to ensure maximum income.

Good health is the foundation of happiness at any age and the requirements of a healthy retirement are discussed in detail — fitness and exercise, diet, sex, your relationship with your doctor.

The essence of successful retirement is preparation and planning. You are never too young to begin thinking about it.

David Loshak, The Health and Social Services Correspondent of *The Daily Telegraph,* believes that Britain is just waking up to the 'retirement explosion' and that our attitudes towards retirement will change dramatically in the next few years. This book will encourage and stimulate all who read it to plan for a successful retirement.